ENGLISH DRAMATISTS

MEDIEVAL DRAMA

Christine Richardson
and
Jackie Johnston

MACMILLAN

First edition 1991

Published by
MACMILLAN EDUCATION LTD
Houndmills, Basingstoke, Hampshire RG21 2XS
and London
Companies and representatives
throughout the world

Typeset by Wessex Typesetters
(Division of The Eastern Press Limited)
Frome, Somerset

Printed in Hong Kong

British Library Cataloguing in Publication Data
Richardson, Christine
Medieval drama.—(English dramatists).
1. Drama in English, 1066–1400. Critical studies
I. Title   II. Johnston, Jackie   III. Series
822.109
ISBN 0–333–45476–6
ISBN 0–333–45477–4 pbk

Contents

Note

While this book is the result of a constant and direct collaboration between the two authors, Part I, Mystery Plays, is the work of Christine Richardson and Part II, Moralities and Interludes, is the work of Jackie Johnston. The General Introduction was written jointly.

Editor's Preface

Each generation needs to be introduced to the culture and great works of the past and to reinterpret them in its own ways. This series re-examines the important English dramatists of earlier centuries in the light of new information, new interests and new attitudes. The books are written for students, theatre-goers and general readers who want an up-to-date view of the plays and dramatists, with emphasis on drama as theatre and on stage, social and political history. Attention is given to what is known about performance, acting styles, changing interpretations, the stages and theatres of the time and theatre economics. The books will be relevant to those interested in or studying literature, theatre and cultural history.

BRUCE KING

Acknowledgements

The authors would like to express their thanks for permission to use material for this book to the following:
The Council of the Early English Text Society for quotations from *The Chester Mystery Cycle*, R. M. Lumiansky and David Mills (eds), EETS, SS 3 (Oxford, 1974); *Ludus Coventriae*, K. S. Block (ed.), EETS, ES 120 (London, 1922, repr. 1960/1974); *The Macro Plays*, Mark Eccles (ed.), EETS, OS 262 (Oxford, 1969); *The Towneley Plays*, England and Pollard (eds), EETS, ES 71 (Oxford, 1897/1952); Manchester University Press for quotations from Alexandra Johnston and Margaret Rogerson (eds), *Records of Early English Drama, York*, 2 vols (Toronto and Manchester, 1979); *Two Tudor Interludes*, edited by Ian Lancashire (Manchester, 1980); *The Wakefield Pageants in the Towneley Cycle*, A. C. Cawley (ed.) (Manchester, 1958/1971); Penguin Books Ltd. for quotations from *Four Morality Plays*, edited by Peter Happé (Harmondsworth, 1979); *The Imitation of Christ* translated by Leo Sherley-Price (Harmondsworth, 1952); *Revelations of Divine Love* translated by Clifton Wolters (Harmondsworth, 1966); J. M. Dent and Everyman's Library for quotations from *English Moral Interludes*, edited by Glynne Wickham (London, 1976); *Everyman and Medieval Miracle Plays*, A. C. Cawley (ed.) (London, 1956, repr. 1974); the Folklore Society for a quotation from the Netley Abbey Mummers' Play in *Five Mumming Plays for Schools*, Alex Helm (ed.) (London, 1965); The Folger Shakespeare Library for the stage plan of the

Castle of Perseverance; Meg Twycross for the diagram of the York pageant wagon route; David Parry, K. Reed Needles and David Putzel for the plans of the Toronto pageant wagons.

Old English Letters

In some of the quotations from medieval plays used in the book, the medieval letters þ and ʒ appear. þ corresponds to present day 'th' and ʒ to present day 'g', 'gh' or 'y'.

General Introduction

As with so much of the medieval period, our knowledge of the drama of the Middle Ages remains sporadic, vague and frustratingly incomplete. Outside the general problems of the survival of texts in manuscript from this period, it must also be considered that drama itself is a form which does not lend itself to written record or fixture. Much of drama in the broadest sense is spontaneous and transient and cannot be written down even in the present day environment of literacy and the printed word. Even in our current society of books, films, tape and video-recorders it is interesting to review what among the many forms of drama and entertainment is recorded and registered for posterity: theatre plays, television drama, soap opera, films, TV advertisements, alternative theatre, pub shows, comedians' routines, street theatre, school plays, improvisations, festival theatre, satirical reviews, buskers . . . and this is still ignoring almost all of the types of musical entertainment which also involve drama, such as opera, dance theatre, musicals, rock concerts, pop or rock videos and so on. Very often we record only what we feel to be worthy, important or instructive to others rather than the forms of entertainment which we know best and experience most frequently and which very probably reflect our feelings, understanding and organisation of our world in a much more accurate and revealing manner.

'Medieval drama' was doubtless equally multiform and various and the difficulty of recording it and lack of motivation to do so even greater. As a result certain types of dramatic event have been privileged and have survived to represent the medieval drama of which they formed only a part. The great sequences of public drama of the Mystery Cycles survive, at least some of them, because they were considered to have importance in the civic and religious life of the people who played and watched them, and so do the Morality plays which not only had an instructive and therefore publicly approved function but were also performed by organised groups of professional actors with a material and professional interest in recording the texts. Occasional texts from other spheres of medieval dramatic activity have survived, but it should always be remembered that the few examples we do have represent a much greater whole which we can only reconstruct through hints and analogies.

To recapture a drama of this kind so far from our remove requires a considerable effort of the imagination even when texts survive. The celebratory reality of community drama combines a number of purposes and emotions, as it may be commemorative, an escape from the rigid bounds of the socially acceptable, a form of release through humour, a confrontation with fear or a combination of these and other functions. The diversity of purposes is matched by a diversity of forms. The plays which were spontaneous, unscripted and not recorded are an important strand of drama for us to consider here, as their influence cross-fertilised into the vernacular religious plays which have survived.

This book has been divided to deal with the two main areas of surviving medieval dramatic texts, the plays of the organised religious drama: firstly, the Mystery Cycles, and secondly, the Morality plays and Interludes. It is worth pointing out here that this division is based more upon methods of presentation and function of the drama rather than on chronology or evolution. In late fifteenth-century England it would have been equally possible to witness a performance of the York, Chester, Coventry or Towneley-Wakefield Mystery Cycle, *The Castle of Perseverance*, *Mankind*, *Everyman*, *Fulgens and Lucrece*, a Saint's play, a Robin Hood play, a civic pageant for a royal entry into a city, a liturgical play during the church service, a Mummers' Play or a trickery or misogyny-based turn performed by a solo actor or touring group of entertainers. It should not be thought that one kind of drama died out and evolved into or was substituted by another and it should be borne in mind that all types were thereby open to influence from one another. We have included a chronological table of dates of plays at the end of the book to enable readers to appreciate both the simultaneity and the variety of forms in the medieval period.

The period between the fall of the Roman Empire in the fifth century, with the consequent decay of the Roman theatres, and the early fifteenth century, when the texts of the Mystery plays and Saints' plays begin to appear, supported a varied and lively dramatic activity, even though it is almost void of surviving texts. Although no texts survive, evidence may be gleaned from details contained in Church prohibitions, mentions in letters and writings of the clergy who regularly condemned such performances as well as through the various household accounts and town records where payments are recorded to demonstrate a wide variety of informal dramatic entertainment. Travelling players, known as *mimi, ludatores, ioculatores* or *histriones*, provided dramatic entertainment as they visited towns, villages, courts and monasteries. Mimic performance could include juggling, stilt-walking, ventriloquism, magical tricks and sleight of hand, dancing and performing animals. There was a tremendous range of activities undertaken by these early professional entertainers. In the same period, within the monastic schools imitations of the dramatic works of classical authors such as Terence were undertaken as exercises in Grammar and Rhetoric as well as for entertainment and religious expression so that some knowledge of formal theatre survived. The Latin plays of Hrotsvitha and Hildegard of Bingen remain in text form from this period.[1]

Within the early medieval period liturgical drama formed a part of religious worship. Liturgical drama never left the Church and it is now accepted by most scholars that there was no evolutionary growth from the Latin plays to the more representational vernacular drama. In fact they seem to have co-existed, and while we do have some very early liturgical play texts, these forms were not supplanted by the Mystery Cycles, but existed well into the fifteenth century and were suppressed in England only with the coming of the Reformation. The high point of activity for liturgical drama was the twelfth century, when the liturgical offices of Easter and Christmas were elaborated upon at some length. The Easter ceremonies of the Visitation of the Sepulchre are the most numerous of the ecclesiastical plays but many texts survive also of liturgical Magi and Shepherds Plays. The performance of the liturgical plays was extremely stylised, being performed by clergy as part of the church service, and they represented a symbolic enactment of the office with ceremonial qualities. The plays were an aid to worship and while it may be that without these Latin plays there would have been no vernacular religious drama, any other evolutionary or imitational debt is very small indeed. It is interesting to note that the Shrewsbury Fragments, parts for liturgical plays which survive in an early fifteenth-century manuscript, appear to display the influence of the Mystery plays, further evidence of cross-fertilisation.[2]

Texts which have survived from northern France as well as a lone English text demonstrate that outside the church, drama was active and highly developed in the early medieval period. The Arras plays of Jean Bodel and Adam de la Halle are evidence of a recognised role for drama within secular life and a high degree of dramatic skill.[3] The fragmentary *Interludium de Clerico et Puella*, written in English despite its title, dates from the mid-thirteenth century and whether intended for solo or duet performance reveals a confident use of mimicry, asides and the complicity of the audience in a satirical setting.[4]

The folk drama which has reached us today in the form of Mummers' plays gives many indications of another important area of dramatic activity in the medieval period. A drama linked to ritual celebration and auspices of fertility of the land, the folk drama also exploited satire and a controlled challenge of authority which in turn may be found in certain areas of the Mystery plays and the Moralities.[5] This is a drama of popular culture, a tradition whose origins pre-date the arrival of Christianity in Britain. These plays have survived through an oral tradition and it is therefore inevitable that their exact form has changed over the years, but there is no reason to doubt that the three main types of folk play which have survived until the present day existed in some form in medieval times. These three are traditionally distinguished as the Hero Combat, the Sword Dance and the Wooing Ceremony. The Hero Combat play involves the vaunting and fighting of champions, a death, lamentation, revival by a quack doctor, and a quete, or collection. The same events in the Sword Dance take the form of the dancers weaving their swords in a circle about the neck of one man, the fool, to cause his death. The doctor then revives him and a quete follows. The Wooing Ceremony has as its crucial action a marriage celebration which is preceded by the claim, and its refusal, of a potential husband by an old hag with a baby. Richard Axton has commented that the plays make mockery of birth, marriage and death, thus liberating these basic human events from the normal constraints placed upon them. Their method of combining aggression and distortion provides a kind of 'social catharsis' for their communities. It is not surprising to find that the motifs, the verbal formulae and the roles of this folk tradition sometimes occur within the Mystery and Morality plays. The episode of the quack doctor also appears in the Croxton *Play of the Sacrament*.

The Robin Hood plays, which seem to have flourished in the early sixteenth century, contemporary with the Morality plays and Interludes, are a development of this celebration of natural force and disruption of imposed order. The three texts which have survived, two from late in the period when they were preserved and neutralised by printing, are still characterised by aggression and disruption in the fights and challenges between Robin Hood, the Potter and the Monk.[6]

Another medieval vernacular play form, often underrated in its importance, is the Saint's play.[7] Few of these survive in textual form, doubtless due once again to the effects of the Reformation, but we do know from records that there were many plays of saints' lives, including St Nicholas, Christiana, Clara, Feliciana, Margaret, Sabina, Susanna, Swithin, James, John and Thomas the Apostle. There is a Cornish play of St Meriasek for which we retain the text and two English Saints' plays, those of Mary Magdalene and St Paul, both in the same manuscript (Digby 133). These plays are based on accounts of saints' lives derived from legendary sources, but they also use elements associated with the Morality play, including figures such as the Seven Deadly Sins, for example.[8] Similar in type to the Saints' plays is the Croxton *Play of the Sacrament* which has as its didactic purpose the promulgation of the doctrine of transubstantiation of the host. This play is unique in English, though in some ways similar to Saints' plays, and is based on a miraculous event, performed by the slick manipulation of special effects.[9] At York, as well as the Corpus Christi Cycle plays, there seems to have been a Pater Noster Play and a Creed Play for which unfortunately no texts survive. Hypothesis would suggest that these too were lengthy sequences of short units dealing with different aspects of the prayer and the creed and possibly similar dramatic creations also existed in other cities.

In addition to these forms of dramatic activity, at the upper levels of the social scale the courtly society of medieval times also had its own entertainments. Glynne Wickham has recorded the many events performed by amateurs for the entertainment of their peer groups or for a special visitor.[10] The elaborate 'Entries' staged by many cities to welcome a royal visitor represent yet another source of dramatic expression and influence. The spectacle provided by the representation of mythological or biblical scenes with costly and impressive special effects and props such as fountains running with wine or huge model fish must have inspired staging methods and expectations for the performers and audiences of the Mystery plays and Moralities. 'Disguisings' and carnival celebrations, visits of Lords of Misrule and the Abbot of Unreason also offered alternative dramatic activity and influence.

It is unfortunately not within the scope of this book to investigate all these many forms of medieval dramatic activity and we have reluctantly concentrated only on those forms for which most texts and details of performance survive. In doing so, however, we have always kept in mind the other types of dramatic expression which were current in the period and attempted, when there is evidence of their influence, to relate these to the surviving Mystery, Morality and Interlude texts. It is also impossible to present all the surviving texts even of these representative parts of medieval drama. Because of the essential differences in the form and function of the Mystery plays and the Moralities and Interludes, the two sections of the book have been organised in different ways.

The first Part deals with the Mystery or Corpus Christi Cycles, beginning with a general introduction to this form of drama, looking at its development, its methods of staging, the function it had in the organisation of its historical time and geographical place and in the spiritual life of players and spectators alike; thus exploring its relationship to its audience and its representation of their lives. The next four chapters each deal with a specific play, using it to talk about its host cycle in general and that particular type of play within the other cycles, as well as discussing certain concepts of medieval dramatical communication which it displays.

The choice of plays has been made in order to create a representative mini-cycle, taking one play from the Old Testament section of the cycle, the Nativity sequence, the Passion sequence and the concluding Last Judgement. Within this framework the individual play selected has been chosen from among those printed in the most widely used anthology of medieval drama, A. C. Cawley's *Everyman and Medieval Miracle Plays*.[11] The only exception to this is the use of the Chester Last Judgement Play, which does not appear in Cawley's selection, in order to offer one play from each of the four complete cycles, York, Chester, Towneley-Wakefield and N-Town. Even if readers are actually studying a particular play from another cycle it should be possible to draw points of analysis and interest from the chapter which deals with the background and structure of the play, the type of play and examples of the same play in other cycles. Although each chapter is self-contained and may be read individually, it is hoped that the whole section will be referred to even if the reader is principally interested only in the specific individual play under discussion.

The nature of the Morality plays and Interludes requires a different approach. Morality plays varied in scope and size as well as place and conditions of performance. Some were large-scale outdoor affairs, such as *The Castle of Perseverance*, while others, such as *Youth*, were quite short and intended to be performed indoors between courses at a banquet. Importantly these plays were not linked to any particular feast day or celebration and were thus much more flexible in form and less tending to type than the Corpus Christi Cycle plays. They are chiefly distinguished by their use of personified figures who present in didactic form man's fallen nature, his temptation and his salvation. Typical of the plays were the figures of the World, the Flesh, the Devil and the Seven Deadly Sins. The Tudor Moral Interlude was a variant of the Morality play, using many of the same features and motifs for increasingly political and social purposes.

Part II of the book, concerning the Morality plays and Interludes, builds on the concepts introduced in the first section of the book, and as it concerns plays in a somewhat different dramatic tradition – the didactic theatre of moral instruction – it extends the notions of performance analysis and demonstrates the interrelatedness of dramatic forms of the period. The first chapter analyses the form of the Morality play and discusses its function as didactic drama, examining the use it makes of allegory. This chapter focuses particularly on what is often erroneously considered the 'typical' Morality play, *Everyman*, and compares it with the *Castle of Perseverance* and *Pride of Life*. There then follows a chapter on the use of space in the staging of Morality plays, with especial reference to the *Castle of Perseverance* and place-and-scaffold staging, showing how movement and reference within the playing area establish a thematic action within the play. The third chapter of this part of the book looks at the role of the audience and the exploitation of humour and elements from popular entertainment and folk drama as part of a moral intention for the plays in *Mankind*. A further chapter focuses on the changes in the role of identity and naming from the earlier Morality plays to the later Tudor plays where this reflects the growing importance of social and political concerns in Tudor society. The final chapter examines the two strands of sixteenth-century drama, popular and elite, dealing with the use of doubling (i.e. actors taking two parts), the Vice figure and the development of the playing area. John Bale's plays, *The Pardoner and the Friar*, *Gammer Girton's Needle*, *Ralph Roister Doister*, *Hickscorner* and *Horestes* are the examples discussed.

The book as a whole is as concerned with the stage as with the page and the study of performance is located in an active stage-centred reading of the text. It must be emphasised that this is intended to provide the reader with a way of thinking the text into theatrical contexts, rather than as a survey of specific productions. A simple distinction must be made between the dramatic or written text and the performance text of possible realisation. While acknowledging the importance of working from performance to dramatic text, it is the case so often for the medieval period, with no recorded contemporary performances and few modern productions to work on, that for the most part we have to work from dramatic text towards stage contextualisation, as the opportunities to work in the opposite direction are very few. However, these opportunities given by modern reconstructions of early plays have been taken when they arise. The reader should at all times be aware that a theatre historian or dramatic critic can only make suggestions and help to pose informed or challenging questions. It is to be hoped that the suggestions and questions explored within this introductory book will stimulate readers to find out more about medieval drama and the critical and performance possibilities it offers, to read more plays, to visit performances of medieval plays and to stage their own productions.

PART I
Mystery Plays

1
Mystery Plays

During the fourteenth and fifteenth centuries the dominant type of formal theatre in England was the Mystery Cycle. In many of the larger cities a series of short plays on episodes from the Bible were performed sequentially outdoors, during one day in early summer, by members of the trade guilds, for the delight and instruction of the general public and the prestige and renown of the guild and its members. The audience was free to come and go from the performance in the absence of formal theatre buildings and admission charges. Many of the 'actors' performing the plays were known to the audience either personally, as friends, neighbours, relatives or professionally, as butchers, tailors, builders, etc. and the performances took place on a day when the normal activities of work and trade were suspended for the holiday of which the plays formed part. The plots of the plays were well known to the audience and there was no suspense involved as to the final outcome. Many, if not all, of our contemporary conventions and expectations of plays and play-going were absent or directly inverted. This was not the only form of drama available in the period, but it received the most financial attention and creative commitment from those who performed it and the most official attention and approval from both civic and religious authorities who provided a physical, temporal and moral space for it to play in and supported the themes it promoted. This kind of drama lasted for at least two hundred years.

Obviously in such a long period the Mystery Cycles underwent many changes and developments and our understanding of them today is necessarily sketchy and general. As the texts of the plays which have survived date from the later period of their development we have a slightly biased view of the Mystery Cycles and can often only hypothesise as to the earlier forms and functions. Even from the later period documentary evidence is scarce and we have only very limited and incomplete records of both the staging and the context of the Mystery Cycle plays. From the details we do have, however, contained in guild records, in civic documents and in the texts of the plays themselves, a picture can be put together of the Mystery plays.

The plays were performed generally as part of the celebrations for the Feast of Corpus Christi and are therefore sometimes known as Corpus Christi plays. Corpus Christi is a religious holiday which was instigated in 1311 to celebrate the doctrine of Transubstantiation, that is, the symbolism in the Mass of the Host which is taken in communion as the body of Christ – 'corpus Christi'. The Corpus Christi Feast celebrates the possibility of salvation through the sacrifice of Christ at the Crucifixion made available to all through communion in the Christian Mass. The Feast is held on the Thursday after Trinity Sunday and can thus fall any date between 23 May and 24 June, the period of early summer in England when the weather is most likely to be fine, there are long hours of daylight and the mood is most likely to tend towards holiday and entertainment rather than work. Importantly, this is a period of the year which was already strongly associated with folk celebrations and festivals culminating in the pagan Midsummer Festivals on June 23rd and 24th. The Church was thus able to exploit the positive holiday mood of the season and to apply it to a religious celebration, expressing the uplifting, joyous possibility of Salvation after the darker mood of the Easter celebrations. As dramatic representations had often been associated with the folk festivals, expectations of some kind of drama were already associated with the period.

Initially the Corpus Christi Feast was celebrated with a Procession through the streets of the town, carrying the Host in its ornate container, accompanied by the religious and civic authorities and the members of the trade guilds dressed in their best clothes and carrying the banners of their guild. It is not precisely known when or how this procession grew into a performance of plays but it would seem that by the second half of the fourteenth century the guilds had added representations of biblical characters or episodes to the banners they carried in procession, as was already the custom for civic processions and 'entries'. For such entries, which were held to honour the arrival of royalty or the powerful nobility in a town, the noble visitors' party would be met at the gates of the city by the Mayor and counsellors and accompanied through the streets to the Town Hall, passing tableaux vivants of townspeople dressed as historical, biblical or mythological personages. Sometimes these tableaux were merely pictorial and involved no movement or speech from their living component parts, though sometimes set speeches were given. It seems likely that in the desire to make their individual contribution to the Corpus Christi Procession more interesting and to draw more attention to their guild through ingenuity and display, the guild members gradually elaborated their representations into what became short plays. Once the Procession had become encumbered with these more lengthy and complicated scenes, it would have had to halt at intervals so that they could be performed. The records from York indicate that, perhaps in response to such a development, the Procession was separated from the Guild plays and was ordered to be held on the following day, probably to leave more room for the plays themselves and to restore the religious awe and devotion which was due to the procession of the Host and which had become overshadowed by the plays.[1]

The subjects for these plays were provided from episodes connected with the initial motivation of the Feast and Procession, the sacrifice of Christ. The Passion of Christ was an obvious sequence to be illustrated, but it was necessary to extend this to cover also the ultimate result of this sacrifice in the Day of Judgement or Doomsday, when all humankind would be judged and either saved or damned for eternity, according to the choices they had made in response to Christ's teaching and sacrifice. The early incidents of the Life of Christ portraying the Nativity, which formed an obvious prologue to the Passion, similarly provoked a retrospective urge to completion which brought in the episodes relating to why the Birth and sacrifice of Christ were necessary, thus to the Creation and Fall of Man. Other episodes from the Old Testament were included according to the principle of typology which was a dominant mode of biblical interpretation in the medieval period. Characters or incidents in the Old Testament were seen as types prefiguring Christ or the sacrifice of Christ as a way of demonstrating both the inevitability of Christ's Birth and sacrifice and the part it played in God's predestined plan for Christianity. Noah could be considered as a 'type' of Christ for he had saved the (good) world from destruction with the Ark during the Flood; Abraham and Isaac prefigured the sacrifice of Christ for Abraham was a father who was prepared to sacrifice his son as God would later sacrifice His Son. By the time of the Mystery Cycles, typology had already been used widely in patristic writings, scriptural interpretation and the arts, where it formed an organisational principle in manuscript illumination, sculpture and stained glass. It was therefore a universal common part of the individual's understanding of the Bible, for the audience as well as the actors and creators of the plays.

The cycle consisted of a series of plays on Christian history, usually beginning with the Creation of the World, moving through episodes from the Old Testament prefiguring Christ to the Birth, Ministry and Passion of Christ, the Resurrection, Harrowing of Hell and Day of Judgement. Plays on the life of the Virgin were often included although these were suppressed in the mid fifteenth century during the Reformation. After being revived during the reign of Mary Stuart, the Marian plays were suppressed again, as eventually the whole Mystery Cycles were, with the return to Protestant order under Elizabeth I. Comparing the surviving cycles and records of lost cycles, Kolve has suggested that an essential 'skeleton cycle' would have consisted of plays on the Fall of Lucifer, the Creation and Fall of Man, Cain and Abel, Noah, Abraham and Isaac, the Nativity, Lazarus, the Passion and the Resurrection, and Doomsday.[2] Most cycles had considerably more than these skeletal incidents. Other Old Testament episodes could be inserted and the Nativity almost always divided up into several plays dealing with the Annunciation, the Visit to Elizabeth, Joseph's Trouble, the Journey to Bethlehem, the Annunciation to the Shepherds, the Magi, the Flight into Egypt and the Slaughter of the Innocents. In the same way the Passion consisted of many separate incidents which could form individual plays to show the Entry into Jerusalem, the Last Supper, the Garden of Gethsemane, the Trial before Pilate, the Trial before Herod, the Buffeting and the Crucifixion. As they have come down to us, the texts of the surviving four cycles[3] indicate that the York Cycle consisted of 49 plays,[4] the Towneley-Wakefield Cycle of 32, the Chester Cycle of 25 and the N-Town Cycle of 41. However, the lists of plays which survive from Beverley, Norwich and Newcastle and the records which survive from Coventry indicate that considerably shorter cycles were held in these places. It is even possible that the Coventry Cycle consisted only of New Testament material.

The individual plays, or pageants, are relatively short with a running time of between 15 and 30 minutes. They were played in sequence on wagons which served as movable stages in the street. According to records from York in particular it would seem that the wagons followed a pre-fixed route through the town, stopping at predetermined 'stations' where they would perform the play. In York at least there would have been ten or twelve stations, so that each play would have been performed ten or twelve times each year. Some critics have disputed that it would have been physically possible to encompass this method of performance within the bounds of one day. A rough mental calculation of 49 plays lasting an average 20 minutes each played at ten stations does indeed suggest an impossibly long performance time. However, it must be remembered that while one play was performing at one station, other plays would be performing simultaneously at the other nine stations. The records from York are quite clear that the plays were performed in this way and both the instructions to the guilds to assemble their plays ready to begin at 4.30 a.m. at the first station and to waste no time moving from station to station and the list of the actual stations still survive.[5] With this manner of performance the final play, the Day of Judgement Play performed at York by the wealthy and influential Mercers' Guild, would have been performed in darkness at the final station. This would have provided a spectacular and impressive close to the cycle especially appropriate to the didactic message of this play, which urged the spectators to repent and lead blameless lives lest they be condemned to eternal agony in the Hell vividly portrayed and described in the play.

Not necessarily all the plays of the cycle would have been performed every year. Not all the guilds were wealthy enough to bear the considerable expenses of producing their play every year and in times of economic difficulty the guild may have preferred to pay the fine to the City Council for not 'bringing forth' their play rather than incur the much higher costs of production. In 1535 in York, although the cycle was eventually not performed, records show that only 35 of the guilds had been preparing their pageants. Sometimes two plays were amalgamated as two guilds joined forces to produce them, and there is some evidence to suggest that two plays may have been performed together at the stations 'in tandem' and this too would have reduced the potential lengthy playing time of the cycle.[6]

The pageant wagons were wooden flat-topped carts, usually with four wheels, that were most probably pushed and pulled from station to station by men rather than horses. Guild records often refer to payments for beer for the wagon bearers. The playing area consisted of the floor of the wagon, the ground in front of it and often an upper storey constructed on the wagon itself which was used to represent Heaven and to provide a playing space for God and Angels. The wagons were very probably curtained to provide both a backdrop and an inner space in which characters could be discovered. The wagons were usually decorated elaborately and guild records show frequent payments for painting the wooden rims of the wagon and the wheels. Painted boards or cloths may have been hung from the sides or the front of the wagon stage to cover the space between the wagon floor and the ground, and perhaps to allow a method of presenting devils from below in contrast to the angels from the upper level. Some pageants had a smaller secondary wheeled structure which provided an additional playing area. The Mercers' Pageant at York had a smaller structure which represented Hell Mouth.[7]

Scenery on the wagons was probably minimal and the playing space was purely representational. Characters refer to the space as a stable or a throne room to identify it rather than relying on the scenery and props to produce a realistic image of such places. Only when scenery or props were essential to the stated action of the play would they have been included. The Norwich Adam and Eve Play records make mention of purchases of fruit to hang on the Tree of Knowledge from which the serpent persuades Eve to pluck an apple and the Cross on which Christ is stretched and bound in the Crucifixion plays would have been an actual wooden structure. In the Chester Herod Play, stage directions indicate that Herod in his raging gesticulates wildly with a staff and breaks a sword in his fury.

Pageant Wagon Reconstructions   York Cycle Toronto 1977

YORK CYCLE '77
Wagon Box Design
series I Anno 77
K Reed Needles   Wagon 5 Gold "Dolphin"

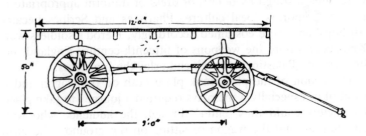

YORK CYCLE '77
Curtain Frame
Position
Anno 77

K Reed Needles

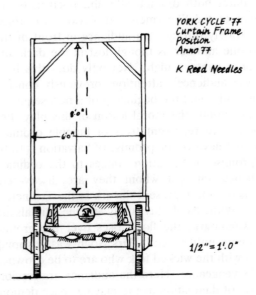

1/2" = 1'. 0"

Costumes were usually fairly elaborate and guild records reveal
that money was frequently spent to replace or repair them.
Unfortunately, precise details of the costumes are not given in the
records where they are described in general terms as 'a cote for
God', 'gloves', 'hose' and so on. As in all medieval art there
would have been no attempt to costume the biblical characters
authentically in either historical or geographical terms. Costumes
were contemporary and distinctions of rank, class or profession
were demonstrated by details of dress or uniform appropriate to
the contemporary local culture. Pharisees and Scribes became
'Bishops' and were costumed accordingly, Herod's soldiers were
Knights and bore the weapons of fifteenth-century England, not
first-century Palestine, with which to slay the Innocents.

The action of the plays took place both on the wagon and in
front of it, especially if the plays required a journey to take place.
Characters could thus 'enter' through the audience who were
standing around the wagon or sitting on the ground. The more
prosperous may have paid for a place on scaffolds erected at the
stations in order to watch the plays in comfort and apart from the
general public. This informal divide between 'actors' and audience
is exploited in the plays both dramatically and doctrinally. In
the Coventry Pageant of the Shearmen and Taylors, the three
Shepherds enter separately through the audience in front of the
wagon and shout to one another as though lost in the dark and
mist of the moors on a winter's night. Not only does this both
effectively capture the audience's attention, previously concentrated on the wagon, and signal the beginning of a new sequence
in the play, but it also points the moral lesson of this play. For
the Nativity Shepherds are representatives of humble ordinary
people to whom the first news of the promise of Salvation is to be
made, just as the promise of Salvation applies to the ordinary
people of the audience amongst whom they are discovered.
Similarly the wagon is used to represent the ark in the Towneley-
Wakefield Noah Play. While Noah, his family and the animals are
safe on board the wagon-ark, the flood rises over the ground
around the wagon where until recently Mrs Noah was gossiping
on the audience level with the wicked folk who are to be drowned
in the flood as God's vengeance. Here the audience are forcibly
reminded of their risk of damnation as the playing space demonstrates that they are now under the waters of the Flood.[8] The stage

directions of the Coventry Shearmen and Taylors' Pageant indicate that Herod should rage 'in the pagond and in the strete also' so that the full force of his fury should be apparent to the audience. The actors in the plays were mostly members of the guild which produced the particular play. It seems though that especially skilful actors could be hired to perform in another play as well. A statute of 1476 declares that no actor is allowed to perform in more than two plays on Corpus Christi Day and a very heavy fine awaited anyone who was found to have done so. It is easy to imagine the chaos which could ensue if a play were held up in its progress through the stations because one of its actors had gone back to play in a pageant just beginning the route. Presumably the two appearances which were permitted would have been allowed only in one play from the beginning of the cycle and one from the end so that backlogging did not occur. The actors were paid for their performances, those with longer parts receiving more than those with shorter parts. In the mid-fifteenth century the Chester Shepherds were paid 12d. and 18d. for fairly long parts. Trowle, the Shepherds' Boy, was paid more, probably because he had tricks and business to perform which are not recorded in the text.[9] Women did not perform in the plays although they were admitted to the guilds. Their contributions remained the typically domestic ones of washing the costumes and providing food, women's parts in the plays being taken by men or youths.[10] Animals do seem to have been used; there are clear references to horses in the Chester plays and possibly a dog, Dottynolle, in the Chester Shepherds Play. Unfortunately there are no records of the Wakefield Shepherds Plays to indicate if Mak's stolen wether, later disguised as a baby, was a real animal or a prop. It is tempting to think that it was an animal for the comic effect it could thus have produced. Music played an important part in the Corpus Christi plays and professional musicians were hired to perform it. The appearance of God and Angels was probably always marked by music.[11]

The audience for the Corpus Christi plays was involved in the plays in ways which have perhaps never been matched in dramatic performances since. The purpose of the plays was directed entirely towards the audience and the theme of the drama was intended to affect their lives and behaviour. Even with present-day political theatre, which in some ways resembles the medieval cycle plays more closely than any drama in the intervening period does, there is not such a concentration of interest on the audience. The cycle plays were intended to instruct the members of the audience in the tenets of the Christian faith and to lead them, through example, to live their lives in a way which would ensure them eternal bliss rather than damnation. The matter of the plays had a very real relevance to the audience's own lives and the most important role in these plays was taken on not by the author or the actors, as would happen in the Renaissance theatre and again in the nineteenth-century theatre, but by the audience. Despite this important focus of attention, the cycle play audiences were the least formally constrained of any theatre in the ensuing western European tradition. Performances were not in a special building with limited seating capacity, but in the streets and at several locations so that there was a possibility for all to see. No money was required to witness the performance so no economic sacrifices were required on the part of the spectators. The duration of the plays was short and thus required neither lengthy periods of absence from home, children or domestic work nor long concentration. Silence and immobility were not enforced and if a member of the audience was bored or uncomfortable or had another urgent commitment then there was no social stigma incurred or inconvenience caused to other members of the audience by leaving at any point in the performance. A play which had to be missed because it was time to organise the family meal could easily be caught up with at a later station, or even the following year, and the general plot of the play was already known. Martial Rose rejected the practicability of processional staging at several stations because he felt that it would have created 'intolerable strain' for the audience, but in fact this mode of performance is the most relaxed possible for the audience. Performances were not for the wealthy or intellectual elite but for all Christian souls, and even non-Christian souls who might thus be converted.

Audience involvement was also apparent at the organisational level of the cycles. Among the audience, all members of guilds had contributed a small sum of money towards the preparation and performance costs of the pageant and financial contribution to a cause is a very effective means of increasing interest in the endeavour. Even non-guild members may have themselves provided services in repairing the wagon, selling nails or axle grease to the guild, cutting cloth for costumes or pouring beer for the wagon bearers. If an individual spectator had not personally been involved in any of these ways then it was virtually certain that a family member, or friend or associate had been. It must be remembered that medieval cities were small and population very low by present standards. All levels of society were addressed by the plays and while the essential message is clear to all degrees of intellectual sophistication, the plays do contain more elevated consideration of both doctrine and poetry for those who are capable of receiving them. Though the plays functioned very well as books for the unlettered[12] they were also watched enthusiastically by the rich, powerful and educated. It was a matter of considerable social prestige to have a station of the York Plays fixed outside your house and the privilege was bitterly contested. Richard II saw the York Cycle in 1397 and the Coventry plays were seen by Queen Margaret in 1457, by Richard III in 1484 and by Henry VII in 1486 and 1492.

The plays were also seen as an occasion which exalted the honour of both the individual guilds and the city itself. They formed a significant expression of social unity and bonding, reinforcing the social units of craft group and city. The York Ordinance of 1476 refers to the preparation of the players who must be 'sufficant in persoune and conying to the honor of the Citie and worship of the said craftes . . .'.[13] The Coventry plays, according to Dugdale's report, caused a 'very great confluence of people thither from far and near' which 'yielded no small advantage to this city'.[14] The guilds were well aware of the glory which reflected on them from the performance of a fine play and the rivalry between guilds for the 'best' plays was intense. The York Masons were upset that their apocryphal play 'Fergus' cast them into ridicule and petitioned to be given a more respectable play. It has sometimes been suggested that the plays assigned to various guilds afforded the opportunity for craft advertising in that appropriate plays were often performed. Thus the Goldsmiths were often given the play of the Three Kings as they would be able to provide the requisite gold artefacts for the gifts and perhaps encourage orders by displaying their skills in the production of such objects. This is one of the possible explanations for the responsibility of certain guilds for certain plays but certainly not the unique cause. It is never the case that the same guild performed the 'appropriate' play in all cycles and there was considerable swapping of plays between the guilds from year to year. Often the assignment of a play may have been made on the basis of the particular devotion the guild had to a saint, or to the Virgin for example.[15]

It is not known who wrote the cycle plays. In certain cases individual authors can be distinguished in a cycle by style or tone but no names or biographical details can be given. There is no doubt, however, that the cycles were the work of many hands and that they developed, were altered and adapted throughout the years of their performance. The texts we have today represent only the form in which the cycle was at the moment in which it was written down in the manuscript which by chance has survived. It is possible that the cycles in the versions we have today were never actually performed in that precise form. Improvisation and adaptation caused by changes in cast or local events were probably very common and while the basic plot remained the same the dialogue would have varied considerably. Parts would have been learnt and passed on, principally orally, and this too would have led to variations. Many plays demonstrate layers of construction in which alterations and insertions may be distinguished in changes of verse form and rhyme scheme or even contradictory sequences of events. A piece of business from another cycle may have been incorporated into an existing play when one of the cast or the guild had seen it and appreciated it in another city. This appears to be the case with the N-Town Shepherds Play which seems to have had material from the Chester or Coventry Shepherds Play grafted onto it at some stage and the Towneley-Wakefield Cycle has several plays which are close copies of York plays. It is generally agreed that the authors called upon to add to or adapt the plays would have been clerics, because of their literacy and familiarity with the subject matter. The plays never contradict biblical details or doctrine and often reflect standard elements of theological interpretation. The cycle plays were not artistic unities created by a single author but a collaborative and participatory form of dramatic expression.

The Mystery Cycles had three basic threads of motivation and function: they were didactic drama intended to express a moral message that would ultimately save the souls of audience and actors, they were occasions for popular entertainment to provide a pleasant means of passing a day free from work and they were occasions for the expression of civic display, craft honour and local unity. It should not be thought that because the subject matter of the plays is religious, the entertainment and civic elements are secondary. All three threads were integral parts of the drama and their complementary binding was responsible both for the creation of the plays and for their continuation through two hundred years of performance. Many of the elements of this drama which appear contradictory or unexpected to modern audiences can   traced back to this threefold structure. According to present-day expectations the plays are not realistic and are full of anachronism, solemn yet raucous, a disturbing mixture of styles. The concentration of the cycle plays was on the present and their presentation of the biblical material was in terms of its universal significance and its relevance to the contemporary medieval audience. In the plays the past is seen as present and their realism is directed entirely towards establishing the identity of the spectators with the characters portrayed in order to demonstrate their complicity in the evil state of the world and to urge their repentance to share in the Salvation God offers through Christ.

Even though the plays are representational it was nonetheless the supposed blasphemy of men playing God or Christ which aroused the condemnation of them by the new Protestant Church in the sixteenth century and was used as a motivation to suppress the Mystery Cycles. At first the cycles were adapted and offending references to the Virgin Mary were removed, but eventually the Church authorities succeeded in suppressing all the plays. Their technique was to call in the 'originals' – the written version of the complete cycle – for 'examination', to make sure that they contained no Popish material, and then never to release them again for performance. In York, Archbishop Hutton called in the play books for examination in 1575 and despite repeated entreaties from the Council that he should suggest and carry out corrections and then restore the books for performance they were never returned.[16] It is important to remember that at this point of English history, religion was very much a part of politics, and official disapproval of the plays from the heads of the Church could have had immediate and powerful influence on the civic authorities responsible for the production of the Mystery Cycles outside the bounds of theological nicety.

After the suppression of the performances and confiscation of the texts, the Mystery Cycles faded into almost total oblivion. The other forms of drama such as the Morality plays and the Interludes continued to be given and the large number of texts of these dating from the late sixteenth century attests to their growth and success. Spontaneous shows of popular entertainment no doubt continued as before, yet have left no written trace of their form or content. More significantly, in this period, formal playhouses were being set up and indoor fixed-time performances by professional actors were becoming the standard. Memories remained in the Elizabethan theatre of Mystery play performances and particularly of their modes of performance and organisation of the playing space but the plays themselves were never revived. Once those who had taken part in the plays or had seen them were dead, the only references to the performances remained hidden in the guild records and civic papers which were hardly sources of frequent interest or reading matter for later generations. In the nineteenth century the manuscripts of some plays were published in the general awakening of interest in 'antiquarian' matters of that period but aroused scant interest from writers or scholars of literature or drama. The critics of medieval literature turned their attention to the texts of the Mystery Cycles at the end of the last century and the beginning of this, but their interest was first in re-establishing the text from the manuscript and then in rhyme schemes and metre, considering the plays as, in their opinion, poor forms of poetry. Critical attention was also turned to the relationship between the various cycles and to the sources of ideas, theology and apocrypha which they contained.

In the last thirty years, stemming from an influential book by Eleanor Prosser, the plays have been studied as drama and some understanding both of their modes of performance and of the motivation behind these has been established.[17] At present there is considerable interest in discovering all recuperable details on staging methods and details of performance from guild records and civic papers throughout Britain, and at the same time the plays are being performed, not only as academic exercises by students and scholars, but also as festival and commercial theatre. The production of the York Cycle in York as part of the 1951 Festival of Britain celebrations was seminal in this respect, although to a certain extent it set unfortunate precedents and expectations in not attempting to follow authentic staging conditions and in using a modernised text. Productions of this kind have in the last ten years become fairly frequent; the York plays are produced every three to four years in the city, keeping to the 1951 staging and text, and other home cities of cycles such as Coventry and Lincoln have also adopted this type of festival performance. What are more interesting are perhaps the recent attempts to perform the cycles in authentic manner, using wagons and processional staging. The University of Toronto has performed both the York and Chester Cycles in this way and in Britain the University of Leeds has organised authentic stagings of the York, Towneley-Wakefield and Chester Cycles. Although not using authentic staging methods and once again relying on a modernised text, the National Theatre's productions of 'The Mysteries' have brought the cycle plays to the attention of a much wider general theatre public and offered stimulating modern dramatic equivalents for many of the medieval performance modes. The Medieval Players also offer individual Mystery plays as well as Moralities, Interludes, Farces and other types of medieval-inspired dramatic entertainment as commercial theatre. The context in which the Mystery Cycles came into being and flourished can of course never be recreated since society, religion, labour and the individual have moved on from the medieval situation. However, attempts to reproduce authentic staging conditions and explore medieval modes of dramatic expression can lead to interesting discoveries about the nature of drama and the possibilities of performance, while searches for modern equivalents to the medieval methods and referents can recreate the effect of the Mystery Cycles in their own time.

The survival of manuscripts from the medieval period is often an arbitrary and hazardous process. The texts of the Mystery Cycle plays were particularly prone to non-survival due to their content, which was officially suppressed by the Church, and their form, acting copies which may have been consumed by use or been kept by many individual actors, as well as facing the ravages of time, damp, worms, mice, fire and reuse for binding or scribbling. Records of plays or performances were likely to suffer the same treatment and so today we have only four surviving complete cycles (York, Chester, Townley-Wakefield and N-Town), one partial cycle (Coventry), two individual cycle plays (the Newcastle Noah Play and the Norwich Adam and Eve Play), four lists of cycle plays (Newcastle, Norwich, Beverley and Ipswich) and references to cycle performances in several other cities from which no texts or lists survive (London, Lincoln, Canterbury, Preston, Kendal, Lancaster, Louth).[18] It is almost certain that in the fifteenth and sixteenth centuries there were many more cycles than these records would suggest.

The bulk of the surviving texts and records comes from north and eastern England. Some critics have taken this to indicate that the Mystery Cycles were unknown in the south of the country. Since there are records of cycles in London and Canterbury this would not appear to be the case, and it is perhaps simply the result of better manuscript preservation in the parts of the country which were less politically and intellectually active in the following centuries.

2
N-Town 'Cain and Abel'

Of the four surviving complete cycles of Mystery plays, the N-Town Cycle is in many ways the most problematical and the least typical. Whereas the other cycles and indeed the single plays can be confidently ascribed to a particular geographical location and can supply indications of their manner of performance, this cycle reveals no certain details about either provenance or staging. It is in addition a structurally complex cycle which shows layers of compilation of very diverse material so that most analytical hypotheses will prove contradictory when applied to the entire cycle. For this very reason, it is perhaps the most challenging of the four great cycles and offers interesting possibilities for hypothetical reconstructions of the performance conditions and for discovering a variety of medieval staging techniques and dramatic solutions.

The N-Town Cycle text is preceded by a Proclamation or Banns which sets out a summary of the plays it contains and which it promises will be performed 'A Sunday next . . . At vj of þe belle . . . In N. town'.[1] The 'N.' is the conventional abbreviation for 'nomen' (name) which was used in blank deeds to stand for a precise name to be filled in later in much the same way that 'x' is now used. It is from this that the usual name of the cycle derives, although sometimes it is also referred to as *Ludus Coventriae*, a confusing and incorrect title which originated in the cataloguing of the manuscript three hundred years ago when it was thought to be the Coventry Cycle. The true Coventry Cycle has since been discovered, at least the two remaining plays of it, and is entirely distinct from the N-Town plays in form, style, language and content.[2] Because of this provision in the Banns for any name of a town to be inserted it is thought that this cycle was perhaps performed in more than one location and did not belong specifically to one place as did the cycles of York, Chester and, very probably, Towneley-Wakefield. It may thus have been a touring cycle and its language suggests the area of East Anglia and Lincolnshire as a potential range of provenance.

Several critics have attempted to prove that the N-Town Cycle is the Lincoln Cycle of Mystery plays which is referred to in records of Lincoln Cathedral and Common Council as well as in some Lincoln trade guild records, but although their suggestions and the evidence they offer are very persuasive there is not yet any definite proof that 'N-Town' should really be 'Lincoln'.[3]

Because of the lack of a firm home town for the cycle, details of staging cannot be drawn out from civic and trade guild records as they can for York and Chester, but must come from the plays themselves. In this respect, though far from presenting complete, unambiguous and detailed stage directions, this cycle does present far more internal indications of staging than do the other cycles. On the basis of the stage directions Cameron and Kahrl have suggested a division of the cycle into three structural layers. They posit a 'proto-cycle' of older plays with infrequent stage directions in Latin, covering the Old Testament plays, the early Life of Christ and a Passion sequence, to which have been added two later 'sub-cycles' with more frequent stage directions in English, one on the Life of the Virgin and the other a Passion sequence. A certain number of plays with stage directions in English and Latin represent the adaptation of older plays to form links to the newly-grafted material and present a more unified sequence.

The stage directions in the I Passion refer quite clearly to 'stages' and 'scaffolds' and instruct characters to go down and walk about 'the place'. Locations are indicated as Annas' stage, Caiphas' scaffold, a little oratory 'as it were a cownsel hous', a 'castle' where the Ass and her foal are, Simon's house, Mount Olivet with 'a place like a park' close by, Mary's house. The 'houses' would seem to be curtained for as the action passes from one incident to another the scaffold 'suddenly uncloses'. Christ riding on an ass enters Jerusalem through the place where he is met by citizens and children with flowers. A particularly dramatic moment of the play is achieved through use of this multiple-location staging when during the Last Supper Christ and the Disciples continue eating while Judas 'rises privily and goes into the place'. Here he confesses his intention of betraying Christ to the audience and then makes his way to the Jews in their house where he agrees to sell Christ for thirty pieces of silver and then 'goes in subtlely where he came from'. After the Jews arrange the details of the ambush the scaffold of the Last Supper 'suddenly uncloses' again and Christ expounds the symbolism of transubstantiation in the bread and wine which represent His body and blood. In this sequence the action freezes on the scaffold as dramatic attention shifts to the place and then recommences as the interest returns to that location and those characters.

This type of simultaneous multi-locational staging is particularly suited to a series of continuous plays where the events logically run on one from another. The Passion sequence has this unity of action for the events are supposedly sequential in both time and place. This is not generally characteristic of the Mystery Cycles, however, which present a series of plays which are sequentially connected by theme and symbolic prediction rather than by unity of time and place. The Passion sequence is central to the cycle, of course, and provides the destination for the symbolic links of the earlier plays and the causal links for the later plays, yet the Old Testament plays would have no dramatic logic if played in a simultaneous staging environment for there is no need for their characters to meet with one another or for their action to take place in the same locations. Adam, Noah and Moses, for example, are linked together symbolically as types of Christ, but can have no direct contact with or use of the same secondary characters in the action of their plays.

Although the place-and-scaffold staging is particularly effective for the Passion sequence it is less so for other sections of the cycle and this has led some critics to feel that certain portions of the cycle were performed in the more typical Mystery Cycle style of single-location wagon staging, introducing the wagon to the general multi-locational setting, using it for individual plays and then rolling it out again. While this hypothesis is not impossible, it is obviously less satisfying than the hypothesis of the whole cycle being performed in the same fashion and this in turn has suggested to some critics the idea that the entire cycle was never performed as a whole but that sections of it were performed separately in different performance modes, perhaps on different days or in different years. The idea of a touring cycle would fit conveniently here for whereas it would be extremely cumbersome to tour elaborate pageant wagons around the countryside, the scaffolds for the multi-locational simultaneous staging of the I Passion sequence and the Marian plays would be much easier to set up in different towns or villages. The prologue to the II Passion sequence given by Contemplacio which refers to the intention 'to procede the matter that we left last year' strengthens the hypothesis of a divided reduced cycle given in succeeding or alternate years, in different places.

It seems clear that the N-Town Cycle is a composite cycle which shows attempts to render it as a coherent whole by the insertion of linking passages but which nonetheless retains a visible variety of staging methods. The Old Testament plays of the cycle certainly appear to be intended for a simpler mode of staging than that of the Passion sequences and have none of the elaborate or detailed stage directions to indicate either specific actions or place-and-scaffold structures. What seem to be later interpolations suggest an attempt to link the first four plays more closely, perhaps to fit them to a place-and-scaffold type staging.

The Cain and Abel Play, the third play in the Old Testament sequence, stands at the centre of this attempted linking. A link is made to the preceding play of Adam and Eve in Paradise by the addition of a brief scene between Cain and Abel and their father Adam. This episode is not strictly required for the traditional Mystery Cycle use of the Cain and Abel sequence which concentrates on the murder of Abel by Cain as related in Genesis IV,1–15. Its existence seems therefore to be justified simply as a means of linking one play to another by use of a common character, Adam. The unusual episode of Cain being killed unknowingly by the blind Lamech which is interposed between the two sections of the following Noah Play links the Cain and Abel Play to this, again by use of a carry-over character. Typology justifies the insertion, for Lamech's murder first of Cain, and subsequently of the Boy, an utterly unjustified murder, demonstrates the evil state of the world which God is about to punish with the Flood, saving only Noah and his family. The incident in turn connects with and emphasises the continuity of Cain's crime in the fallen world, for Lamech's Boy is an innocent victim as Abel was Cain's innocent victim and, of course, as Christ will be an innocent victim. As Cain's murder of Abel demonstrated the consequences of the Fall, Lamech's murder of Cain demonstrates the proliferation of the act across the world. If Lamech might possibly have been excused because he is blind and thus shot Cain unintentionally, the fully intentional murder of his Boy, on whom he places the blame, is entirely inexcusable. The story of Lamech is apocryphal and is not mentioned in the Bible. The Mystery plays, like all other kinds of medieval religious art, incorporated such episodes as they had been transmitted through exegesis and accorded them equal respect with the orthodox biblical facts when they demonstrated relevant moral points.

In all four of the existing complete cycles the Cain and Abel Play is included as one of the Old Testament plays. Its place in the cycle is assured both for what it represents in its own action and for what it symbolises or prefigures with respect to the movement of the cycle towards the Passion. The murder of Abel by Cain demonstrates the practical consequences of the Fall and gives concrete meaning to the otherwise abstract sin of plucking the fruit from the Tree of Knowledge. It is a demonstrable effect of the Fall in terms recognisable to everyday people. Although Adam and Eve are exiled from the Garden of Eden and promised a life of toil and suffering as punishment for their disobedience, their sin, though serious in theological terms, remains one with which it is not easy for the individual Christian going about his or her everyday life to identify. Cain's sin is much more easily grasped and recognisable to all levels of a medieval audience. Before Adam and Eve ate the apple there was no sin, after the apple, away from Paradise, sin becomes possible and the first sin committed is the most heinous: murder. In this way the Cain and Abel episode follows naturally from the Adam and Eve Play and is almost a necessary conclusion to it. The Chester Cain and Abel sequence in fact forms part of a longer Fall of Man Play which includes the Creation and the Fall and demonstrates very effectively how the Cain and Abel episode is a continuation and completion of the Fall of Man.

On the typological level, Cain and Abel gains its place in the cycle as it had already gained its place in exegesis, sermon and the visual arts because Abel can be seen as a type of Christ. Like Christ, Abel is an innocent victim who is killed by the fallen world, here represented by Cain, as at the Crucifixion the unbelieving Jews represent the fallen world. Abel is also killed by his brother and Christ, who had chosen to appear in the world in the form of a man, born of a woman, is also brother to those who kill Him. The typological analogy can be taken still further in that Abel is the son of Eve, the woman responsible for the Fall, and Christ was the son of Mary, the woman responsible for the Salvation of the world. The Eve–Mary parallel was a favourite contrast in medieval theology which saw Scriptural approval for the balance in the words of the salutation of Mary at the Annunciation when Gabriel addressed her 'Ave Maria, gratia plena' (Hail Mary, full of grace). 'Ave' is 'Eva' backwards and thus Mary was considered to be, even on linguistic grounds, the inversion of Eve, she who would save the world rather than she who had lost the world. The N-Town Salutation and Conception Play which recounts the Annunciation expressly states this inversion:

> Ave maria gratia plena Dominus tecum
> Heyll fful of grace god is with the
> Among All women blyssyd art thu
> here þis name Eva is turnyd Aue
> þat is to say withoute sorwe ar ȝe now.
> (Play 11, ll. 217–20)

Typology was a means of comprehending the unity and purpose of Christian history and of showing that all events formed part of God's plan for the universe. Though many of the events of the Old Testament could be seen to have a cause and logic in their own historical circumstances, nonetheless they also contained a relevance to the Life of Christ and the establishment of the Christian religion which only becomes apparent long after the events themselves. In this way Christianity could incorporate Jewish history and could make the Judaic Old Testament its own. With enough exercise of the interpretive imagination and with no need to insist that one interpretation should not contradict another, practically any event in the Old Testament could be shown to be a type or figure of events in the New Testament. Working backwards from what you wanted to have been predicted, it was fairly simple to manipulate previous events to foretell exactly that, in much the same way that horoscopes often appear amazingly accurate when read after the period of prediction. It is a reassuring and satisfying method of interpreting the world for it suggests that all is ordered and has a function even if it is not immediately apparent. Chaos and confusion can be kept at bay and what may seem painful or disturbing events in the present can be reconciled with the knowledge that they have some greater positive meaning in a larger organisation of the world. During the medieval period typological interpretation of the Bible was a conventional organising principle and was apparent in many spheres of religious life, not merely at an abstract level of intellectual sophistry. It should not be thought that expecting the uneducated, illiterate medieval individual to recognise Abel or Noah or Isaac as a type of Christ was expecting an impossibly obtuse degree of intellectual awareness. Sermons frequently presented such interpretations and stained glass and sculpture in churches grouped such figures or events together.

The plays themselves often directly acknowledge the typological links and point out the relevance of their actions to what will follow. In the N-Town Cain and Abel Play, Abel explicitly likens himself to Christ. When he offers his sacrifice he asks God to accept the lamb through His mercy which will later be shown to the world 'in a lamb's likeness' and will 'for man's wickedness . . . die full dolefully'.[4] The Lamb of God, Christ, will be killed to demonstrate God's mercy to the world, as Abel here sacrifices a lamb to beg for that mercy and as Abel himself will be killed. Another connection between Abel and Christ was also seen in their role as shepherds. According to the biblical narrative, Cain toiled the earth as a grower of crops and Abel was a keeper of flocks. The image of Christ as the Good Shepherd is very strong in the Bible and had been very fully expounded by Augustine in his commentaries on John X and repeated by other biblical scholars so that it was very widely known in the medieval period. Although in the N-Town play there is no direct reference to Abel's profession, except implicitly in his choice of 'first fruit' to offer as tithe, in the Chester play this is stated specifically when Adam instructs his sons in their choice of profession.[5]

The medieval interpretation of Cain and Abel's sacrifice to God saw it as a possibility for explaining the custom of tithing and of urging people to follow the custom diligently. Once again this is an example of how the plays express aspects of biblical history in terms which are more immediately recognisable to the audience of their time. All the extant cycles show Cain and Abel offering a sacrifice to God in the form of a tithe, the system whereby individuals were expected to offer a tenth of their income or products to the Church. The system was obviously open to abuse and people were not always convinced that their contribution was being made to the glory of God rather than to the individual enrichment of the local priest. In the medieval period tithing was a source of resentment as the Towneley-Wakefield Cain expresses in that play:

> My farthyng is in the preest hand
> Syn last tyme I offyrd
> (*Mactacio Abel*, ll. 104–5.)

When Cain refuses to listen to both his father and his brother's advice on tithing he demonstrates not only an aspect of his wicked and disobedient character, but also offers a more immediate lesson to the medieval audience who can in this way be encouraged to offer their tithes willingly and promptly lest they too become cursed and outcast by God like Cain.

In the N-Town play, Abel offers the positive example with respect to tithes for he both makes his sacrifice willingly and carefully explains the reasons for doing so to Cain and thus to the audience. Adam teaches both Cain and Abel to offer their first fruits as sacrifice in return for what God has given them through his love and grace (ll. 38–44). Abel accepts the advice and expresses his intention to follow it immediately, showing himself to be a meek and respectful son to both his earthly and his heavenly father. As he offers his sacrifice to God his speech is characterised by the key words 'meekness' and 'good will' (ll. 62–88). Not only does Abel obey his father's recommendation and the law of God, but he does so humbly and readily, accepting that God deserves the best of their produce since it is through God's grace that they have both best and worst. When Cain nonchalantly says that he will seek out his worst sheaf of corn which God can accept or not as far as he is concerned, Abel once again advises him to show 'good will' in his offering and select only the best for God. Cain

refuses to tithe the best of his produce and moreover makes his
tithe unwillingly ('I had liefer go home well for to dine' [l. 52])
and his tithe cannot be acceptable to God.

Cain's objections to tithing the best seem very reasonable and
could be shared by many of the audience who have possibly
thought the same things themselves. Why should God have the
best? God has no need to eat, whereas Cain, who has put the
labour into producing the corn, could appreciate the best sheaf. It
is Abel who attempts to correct Cain's, and the audience's, thinking
once again as he points out the error of applying material terms
to God and shows that the act of tithing is a symbolic way of
showing thanks to God for providing their food, without which
they would perish (ll. 118–21). It comes as a surprise only to Cain
when Abel's offering burns freely as a miraculous demonstration
of its acceptability to God. Although the biblical narrative makes
no mention of burnt offerings and up until this point neither Cain
nor Abel has mentioned that the tithes should be burnt in sacrifice,
the idea of burning the offerings was used often in the Mystery
Cycle Cain and Abel Plays. Burning the offerings gives the occasion
for a spectacular and attention-catching episode which can arouse
admiration for the special effects used to produce it and can
also be clearly seen from some distance away as a concrete
demonstration of the doctrinal point of the acceptability of Abel's
sacrifice to God. In the Towneley-Wakefield play, the point is
further expanded and exploited for Cain and Abel both light their
sacrifices but while Abel's burns well, Cain's makes clouds of
dense smoke which further enrages him and provides more
opportunity for comic choking and so on. While many critics feel
that the more lively Towneley-Wakefield play represents the most
dramatically successful of the Cain and Abel Plays, Eleanor Prosser
considers it an example of gratuitous obstructive comedy which
works against the doctrinal message and dramatic impact of the
play.[6]

Cain and Abel are well contrasted figures in the N-Town play.
Abel is the contemplative and humble figure who seeks advice
first from his earthly father, Adam, and then bends his will to that
of his heavenly Father. He understands the spiritual justification
and importance of his practical actions, the sacrifice of the first
fruits, while Cain remains purely on the physical level and insists
that it does not matter if God is given the best or worst as He will

not even taste it. Abel accepts Adam's instructions to sacrifice the tithe as a demonstration of love, respect and gratitude to God, Cain accepts the idea grudgingly and would rather spend the time in seeking material rather than spiritual sustenance, that is 'go home . . . to dine' (l. 52). Abel shows brotherly concern and mild perturbation at Cain's refusal to follow the lesson of the sacrifice which he painstakingly repeats to him, whereas Cain's reaction to his brother moves from initial jeering through insults to anger, jealous fury and finally murder (ll. 92–156).

The contrast between the two brothers is reflected and emphasised throughout the play in the dialogue, where the difference in their perceptions of good and evil, wise and foolish, is pointed linguistically. For Cain, Abel is a 'fool' (l. 92) and he himself acts 'wisely' (l. 96); Abel's wit is 'feeble' in Cain's eyes. The contrast becomes most marked in lines 118 and 122. Here each brother has the same basic line differing only by the possessive pronoun and the rhyming adjective in final position:

> Yet methinketh my wit is good,
>
> Yet methinketh thy wit is wood,

As the last word of rhymed metrical dialogue gains a special weight from both the rhythm and the rhymes, words in this position have particular importance. In this instance the rhythm of the two lines is identical and the similarity is broken first by the contrasting 'my' and 'thy' and then finally by 'good' and 'wood' (mad). The audience, with the privilege of knowing both the end of the story and the moral lesson it entails, can have no hesitation in recognising Cain's perception as mistaken and accepting Abel's interpretations of good and bad as being correct.

The repetition and contrast is repeated in Abel's speech in lines 135–43 when 'my' and 'thy' contrast again, this time with the opposition of 'the best' (Abel) and 'the worst' (Cain). The difference in the brothers' perceptions of right and wrong is demonstrated in the rhythms of the dialogue as much as in what they say and do. The climax in both contrast and action comes at the point when Cain is prompted to kill his brother through jealousy, the dialogue again stresses the contrast and points out Cain's mistaken perception:

Doth God thee love and hateth me?
Thou shalt be dead, I shall thee slo:
(*Cain and Abel*, ll. 145–6)

Instead of realising that God's acceptance of Abel's offering is a lesson to imitate the form and manner of his tithe, Cain sees it as a motivation to kill Abel. Instead of trying to become like Abel, to follow his example and win God's love, Cain decides to remove Abel and the contrasting model he offers.

The murder is executed rapidly in the space of four lines and Cain expresses verbally what he is performing physically (ll. 149–52). Narration of performance, or deictic comment, is a frequent technique of medieval drama and in addition recalls the folk drama. The champions and challengers of the Hero Combat play of the Mummers' Play tradition almost always describe their actions in the fight. Action and words are fused to give a more profound and incontrovertible meaning to the events. To a certain extent this is required by staging conditions where possibly not all spectators would be able to see clearly what was being performed and would need the reinforcement of verbal description, but the symbolic weight which deixis imparts is an essential element of medieval representation. Medieval plays do not pretend to offer a slice of life or to allow the audience a privileged and unacknowledged witnessing of supposedly real events. Medieval drama 're-presents' the events of biblical history or moral lessons so that the audience can have their understanding reinforced and reconfirmed. It has no space for ambiguous actions. In the same way, characters almost always identify themselves explicitly at the beginning of a play, or are identified by another character. Abel identifies Cain and thereby himself in the third line of the play. The technique can appear artificial and tedious to modern ears, especially in long sequences such as that of the identification of Noah and his family in the Noah Play, but was a conventional feature of the medieval drama closely linked to the medieval idea of representation and the function of drama.

Cain kills Abel with a 'chavel-bone' (jaw bone), as according to apocryphal legend, and then hides his body under a pile of grass or hay (l. 156). This action could well be performed on a pageant wagon where the hay could be already present on the floor of the wagon as a prop, or also in the place of a place-and-scaffold

playing area. In this case it is tempting to assume that there would
have been a small pit in the playing area which could have been
used for hiding Abel's body and which could later in the cycle also
have served as Lazarus' tomb and the burial site for Christ's body.
The jaw bone could have been either a real bone or a special,
possibly larger-than-life, prop bone. The Towneley-Wakefield
Cain kills Abel with a 'cheke-bon' and the Cornish *Creation of the
World* play directs that Abel be killed 'with a chawe bone'. It is
presumably intended to be an animal's jaw bone, as this is the
first death in the world; the *Cursor Mundi* stated that it was an
ass' cheek bone, although dramatic logic suggests in performance
it might have been the sheep's jaw bone from Abel's recent
sacrifice.

When God asks Cain where Abel is, following the murder, Cain
makes the traditional biblical reply that he does not know for he
is not his brother's keeper (l. 161). It is quite apparent to the
audience at this point, and obviously to God who is omniscient
and all-seeing, that Cain is lying. Cain has already demonstrated
his wickedness in his disobedience, to both Adam and God; his
rudeness, to Abel; his uncouth language (l. 144) and of course in
the murder. Here he shows both his disrespect for God and his
arrogance in attempting to deceive God. Throughout the Mystery
Cycle drama, a character's nature and function can be discerned
from their response to the appearance of God or his messengers,
the angels. The response of good characters is always first of fear
and then of humility as God's power is apprehended first physically
then spiritually. The bad characters never display fear but rather
bravado and arrogance. In the Towneley-Wakefield Cain and Abel
Play, Cain responds to God's advice to make a true sacrifice by
pretending to have heard a hob-goblin. He asks who spoke so
quietly, belittling the powerful voice of God's authority and then
claims that 'God is out of his wit'. In contrast, Noah receives
God's instructions to build the ark meekly and humbly asks God
to identify himself; the troubled Joseph, worried about his wife's
inexplicable pregnancy, thanks the Angel who comes to explain
the situation to him for showing concern and interest in his
problems; and the Shepherds at the Nativity are at first alarmed
by the apparition of the heavenly host but then at once agree to
follow their instructions to go to Bethlehem to worship the new-
born Saviour. Cain's bold reply to God therefore clearly establishes

his fault, his role as a bad character and the inevitable fate which
awaits him, for in the Mystery Cycles, as in Christian history,
those who deny or challenge God or God's will are to be damned
forever.

Cain is cursed by God and it seems that the mark is put upon
him. This detail is not given explicit execution in the play but may
be intuited from Cain's words at line 184: 'I dare never see man
in the visage'. There was no need for the play to give any more
attention to the placing of the mark, for the audience would have
been familiar with this detail and possibly the mark itself would
have been represented by a distinctive mark or at least a sign
hastily painted on Cain's face as he turned to face God, away from
the audience, and then shown to the audience as he turned once
more to face them as he made his lamentation and wandered off
to look for somewhere to hide. It is possible that masks were used
and that the 'mark of Cain' was represented by a particularly
hideous mask.[7] The Chester play shows first God's curse of Cain
and then, uniquely in the Mystery play tradition, Cain's repentance
of his sin. Cain is cursed to the seventh generation and before
leaving to wander mournfully through the world, confesses his sin
to Adam and Eve. In contrast the Towneley-Wakefield Cain
remains unrepentant and a braggart to the end, pronouncing a
version of the King's Peace on himself in an, obviously futile,
attempt to escape from the consequences of his crime while not
repenting of it.

At this point in the N-Town play, Cain moves away from
the playing area, whether pageant wagon or place-and-scaffold,
through the audience, trying to avoid contact with them and trying
to hide. The audience becomes the Mankind from whom Cain is
attempting to hide and the immediacy of the cursed character
moving his pitiful way among the members of the audience would
have been an effective means of pointing the lesson of the play to
them. Murderers, rebels against God's will and non-payers of
tithes must shun human society in the life and times of the audience
as much as in Cain's time. Cain uses an intriguing term when he
lists the places he will wander to seek refuge, 'stage'. This is the
earliest use of the word in English and it does here seem to refer
to an elevated playing area so that Cain uses it appropriately only
to the context of the performance in which he is playing, the
scaffolds of the playing area, or the wagons which he is wandering

among.

When Cain moves away from the playing area, Noah enters and the Noah Play begins.[8] After the Angel has instructed Noah on how to build the ark, Noah and his family exit and Lamech, led by a boy, enters. Lamech wants to shoot his bow, though blind, and inadvertently sends an arrow into a 'great bush' behind which Cain is hiding and thus Cain is slain at last. After Lamech has vented his anger by killing his Boy, Noah and his family re-enter, with the ark. It seems fairly certain that this episode is a later addition to the Noah Play which was inserted to provide covering time for the preparation of the ark which was no doubt an elaborate wheeled structure which had to be pushed in. The Lamech incident is an apocryphal legend but the blind man and boy routine formed part of the tradition of popular entertainment in both Britain and France in the medieval period. It may be that when the compiler or performers of the N-Town Cycle found that something was needed to fill a necessary technical gap in the sequence of the plays, a dramatic sketch from secular entertainment which was perhaps already familiar to the audience was chosen to be incorporated with the necessary changes of name and context for the biblical cycle.[9] This is what seems to have happened in other parts of the cycle, especially in the Shepherds Plays as will be seen in Chapter 3 below.

The Cain and Abel Plays from the other cycles show the same episodes of offering a tithe sacrifice to God, quarrelling over the acceptability of Abel's offering and the murder. The Towneley-Wakefield and the York Cain and Abel Plays form entirely separate units performed by separate guilds on a pageant wagon and have no need for linking episodes to other plays to be inserted. Cain's unwillingness to sacrifice his tithe to God which is expressed through ill-humour and mistaken perceptions of physical and spiritual values in the N-Town play is greatly extended for comic and didactic effect in both the Chester and Towneley-Wakefield plays. The Chester Cain carefully selects corn eaten by insects or growing by the side of the road and thus dusty and trampled while the Towneley-Wakefield Cain 'mistakes' his counting of the sheaves so that he chooses the tenth part of his crop only from among the sheaves full of thistles and weeds. The episode is long and humorous as Cain considers each sheaf separately and comments on its condition and whether it would be more useful to God or to himself but although the incident is expanded and elaborated for comic effect the idea of Cain's miscounting had respectable patristic origins and is not a brilliant invention of the Wakefield author for it was first expounded by Augustine.[10]

In both these plays the device of Abel's offering burning immediately while Cain's does not or will not burn is used, again with most comic elaboration in the Towneley-Wakefield play. In both these plays God speaks to Cain and attempts to restrain his wrath and instruct him in correct offering and motivation, as Abel does in the N-Town play, and then Cain lures Abel away from God's sight, so he thinks, with an excuse and murders him.

The York play has survived in an incomplete version, missing two pages in the manuscript. An incident involving Cain's cheeky servant, Brewbarret, has been interpolated at a later stage of composition than that of the true Cain and Abel story. Possibly this was added in imitation of the lively Towneley-Wakefield play which features Pikeharnes as Cain's long-suffering but irrepressible Boy. The Towneley-Wakefield plays in general bear many resemblances to the York Cycle and there was obviously notable and continuing influence between them. Both these Cain and Abel Plays, and also the Beverley play which has not survived, were performed by the Glovers Guild. Cain's rebelliousness is apparent in the N-Town play and in the Towneley-Wakefield play it is openly expressed in terms of a challenge. It is possible that the play was considered appropriate to the Glovers Guild in that they would have been able to provide a leather gauntlet which could have been used in a formal challenge to God or to the Angel by Cain. The York play ends with Cain returning the curse of the Angel in the manner of a return of challenge.[11]

As in all the Mystery Cycle plays, the bad characters seem to have the best parts and the dramatic concentration is always on Cain rather than on Abel. We must be careful here not to allow our modern sympathies to cloud our understanding of medieval play-writing. Bad characters, Satan, Cain, Herod, Pilate, are represented as being irrefutably bad, in violence of language and gesture, blasphemy and raging, striking other characters physically and insulting them, and the audience, liberally. To the medieval audience this method of representation had the function of establishing an identity with these characters yet also, within the larger structure of the cycle, of warning against such an identification. For these characters were known to have committed sins which led them to eternal damnation, a fate which could easily await the audience. Very often the excitement generated by the bad characters serves to accentuate through contrast the qualities of the good characters and to provide a keener positive model. Though Abel neither shouts nor rages and merely repeats the lesson to Cain in brotherly concern, he demonstrates a patience and self-control in the face of Cain's insults and refusal to understand which may provoke the audience to wonder if they could have exercised such control in similar circumstances. Abel's patience in the face of ill-use and lack of comprehension also prefigures the patience of Christ in the Crucifixion sequence where once again the contrast with noisier, more brutal figures is marked and dramatically effective.

3
Towneley-Wakefield 'Secunda Pastorum'

The precise location for the complete cycle of Mystery plays known generally as the Towneley Cycle is not certain. Unlike the non-localised N-Town Cycle, however, there is every indication that the Towneley Cycle was fixed in one town rather than being a touring cycle. The dialect of the plays is quite clearly that of the north-east of England and headings on two of the plays in the cycle, as well as references to local Wakefield places in three others, suggest very strongly indeed that this cycle belonged to the north Yorkshire town of Wakefield.[1] That Wakefield was the home of a complete cycle of Corpus Christi plays is evident from a letter from the Church Commissioners in 1576 which, in response to news that 'in the towne of Wakefeld in Whitsun weke next or therabouts' there was the intention to play 'a plaie commonlie called Corpus Christi plaie which hath been heretofore used there', sets out a firm warning that any material which 'tende to the maintenaunce of superstition and idolatrie or which be contrarie to the lawes of god or of the realme', in other words to the tenets of the new Protestant state religion, will not be countenanced.

The status of the town of Wakefield as a flourishing centre of the cloth trade in the fifteenth century would certainly support the existence of wealth, civic organisation and pride sufficient to have established and financed a cycle of plays. Many of the plays in this cycle bear a strong resemblance to plays in the York Cycle and it may well be that as Wakefield became more prosperous with the

45

growth of the cloth trade in the late fifteenth century, it borrowed and then developed plays from the already established cycle in nearby York. The name Towneley derives from the name of the family who owned the one surviving manuscript of the cycle from the seventeenth to the eighteenth century, and as evidence for a precise location is circumstantial rather than direct, critical caution has prompted the use of this denomination, although the connections with Wakefield are considered by many critics to be convincing enough to support at least a hyphenation to produce the Towneley-Wakefield Cycle.

It would seem that the closeness to York influenced the method of staging of the Towneley-Wakefield Cycle too. The fines to be imposed set out by the Burgess Court in 1556 are very similar to those in the York Memorandum Book and similarly provide hints of performance.[2] Players of the various craft guilds are to be ready with their pageants at 5 a.m. on the day of performance and are to play only in the 'settled' places, the stations set out by the Council. Although there is less direct evidence for processional wagon staging in Wakefield than there is in York, it nonetheless seems highly likely, given the 1556 document, the proximity and influence of York and the nature of the plays themselves, that this was indeed the method of staging.[3]

Within the Towneley-Wakefield Cycle is a group of six plays which show clear signs of having been created by one author. Although the name and biographical details of this author remain unknown, his artistic and dramatic style is clearly identifiable. The plays in question, the *Mactacio Abel*, *Processus Noe*, *Prima Pastorum*, *Secunda Pastorum*, *Magnus Herodes* and *Coliphizacio*, are characterised by a notable degree of dramatic skill in dialogue and characterisation, a lively use of colloquial idiom and proverbial phrases, a readiness to use roughness of language and action to heighten dramatic effect and capture the audience's attention and a tendency to comment on contemporary conditions both for ease of audience identification and as a means of social criticism. These plays are written in a nine-line stanza which is not found elsewhere in medieval dramatic or poetic texts. The author is now known as the 'Wakefield Master' and despite many attempts to give him a name he remains identifiable only through his work. Educated hypothesis would suggest that he was a cleric living in the Wakefield area who undertook a revision of the Towneley-Wakefield Cycle, possibly offering the four complete new plays, *Processus Noe*, *Prima Pastorum*, *Secunda Pastorum* and *Magnus Herodes* and adapting the *Mactacio Abel* and producing additions and insertions in *Coliphizacio* and several others.[4]

The Wakefield Master has been the subject of attention from many historians of the drama and scholars of medieval literature and critical evaluation covers the entire range from hailing him as a dramatic genius, the first English dramatist, to recommendations to redimension his work in the perspective of other medieval plays which may be seen to be just as finely crafted and dramatically effective. Most attention is given to his *Secunda Pastorum* or *Second Shepherds Play* which is to be found in numerous anthologies of drama, medieval or chronological, English or world. For many people this anthologising zeal has meant that *Secunda Pastorum is* medieval drama and remains their only knowledge of the form. Such isolation and adulation is dangerous, for while *Secunda Pastorum* is certainly an intriguing and successful play it is by no means representative. In fact it is an anomalous, atypical medieval play. It is for this reason that the study of the play which follows will view it continually with reference to *Prima Pastorum* and to the other English medieval Shepherds Plays so that more of its representative qualities may be seen.

All the surviving cycles have a Shepherds Play, but the Towneley-Wakefield Cycle is unique in having two Shepherds Plays. A dramatisation of the Annunciation by Angels of the Saviour's Birth to shepherds in the fields around Bethlehem, as recounted in Luke II, 8–20, was made also within the Liturgical Drama where it was frequently found along with the more common Three Maries plays (*Quem quaeritis?*) and the Magi plays. Apart from the appearance of this incident in the scriptural narrative of the Nativity, the importance of the Christmas Shepherds as representatives of both Common Man and Priests assured the sequence a place in the Corpus Christi cycles. But why *two* Shepherds Plays in the Towneley-Wakefield Cycle and both by the Wakefield Master? It has been suggested that the two plays were performed in alternate years or that *Prima Pastorum* closed the performance of the plays on one day and *Secunda Pastorum* opened the performance on the second day of a two-day cycle. This suggestion sees the Shepherds Plays as providing a link between both the days of performance and the subject of the pre-Birth world which precedes *Prima Pastorum* and the post-Birth world which succeeds *Secunda Pastorum* in both the history of the world and the sequence of the plays in the Towneley-Wakefield Cycle. This particular hypothesis gains credibility from the fact that the Towneley-Wakefield Cycle, at least as it exists today, has no separate Nativity Play and represents the Birth of Christ only within the two Shepherds Plays. All the other cycles devote a separate play to the Nativity itself, which usually directly precedes the Shepherds Play. Another possibility which emerges from a comparison of the form and structure of both plays is that *Prima Pastorum* was the initial Shepherds Play which the Wakefield Master wrote and that *Secunda Pastorum* is a later version which developed out of *Prima Pastorum*. Both plays include the strict sequence of the Scriptural events but also provide an extended sequence of the Shepherds' activities before the appearance of the Angel. This sequence is marked by episodes of quarrelling, trickery and complaint which serve to contrast with the subsequent peace and harmony brought by the Saviour's birth both to the world and to the Shepherds themselves as well as underlining the need for the coming of the Saviour to lead mankind to Grace from the disrupted and despairing state of the post-Fall world. Possibly through rehearsal and performance by a group of enthusiastic and skilful actors, the first disruptive sequence of the Shepherds' quarrelsome Feast in *Prima Pastorum* grew into the more developed, and longer, sequence of Mak's theft of the sheep and disguise of it as a baby, a story which author and actors very probably knew from folk-tale.[5] We can never know, of course, but the contribution of actors in the creation of the Corpus Christi plays should not be ignored or underestimated. Annual performance would have meant the opportunity for improvisation or alteration of an initial play text in response to the actors' interests, skill and desire to 'do something different this year' and to the audience's reaction to their additions or extemporisation. Whether both texts were played or whether *Secunda Pastorum* effectively replaced *Prima Pastorum* remains open.

Plays of the Nativity sequence form another grouping within the Corpus Christi cycles, like the Old Testament plays, the Passion plays and the Ministry plays. The Coventry Cycle seems in fact to have presented all the Nativity incidents in one long play, the Shearmen and Taylors' Pageant which includes the Annunciation,

Joseph's Trouble, the Shepherds, Nativity, the Magi, Herod and the Slaughter of the Innocents. With respect to the didactic significance and number of incidents portrayed, the plays of the Birth of Christ are second only to the plays of the Death of Christ. Like the Easter plays, the Christmas plays are full of awe and reverence, but their overall spirit is of adoration, gratitude and happiness rather than the lamentation, guilt and distress of the Passion sequence. Within the structure of the cycle, of course, the Passion plays also have a note of optimism, for it is through Christ's sacrifice that mankind is saved, but the plays themselves stress the cost of that sacrifice and bring to the fore both Christ's suffering and mankind's cruelty. While the Easter plays tend towards tragedy even in their cathartic effect, the Christmas plays are marked more particularly by comedy, for the happy ending they imply for mankind has not yet been marred by the means which will be necessary to achieve it. Comedy is used in the portrayal of the figure of Joseph in the Joseph's Trouble plays as a comic cuckolded husband and even the potential terror of Herod is deflected in the exaggeration of his rage and power to ranting melodramatic effect while in the Shepherds Plays comedy emerges from the characterisation and activities of the Shepherds themselves as they quarrel, feast, trick one another and sing.

The Shepherds represent a unique type of character in the cycle plays which offered a special type of appeal to a dramatist and his actors. They are Bible characters, appearing in Scriptural narrative, but have no names, qualities or actions, apart from receiving the news of the Saviour's Birth and going to worship Him, ascribed to them. Unlike Noah whom the Bible described precisely as old, with three sons, and three daughters-in-law, God-fearing in a time of sacrilege and sin, the Shepherds had no constraints placed on them or preconceptions for the dramatist to use. The Luke sequence does not even say how many Shepherds there were. In the Scriptural narrative the Shepherds represent members of common Humanity to whom the message of Salvation is directed and thus in their treatment in the plays, the dramatist was encouraged didactically to develop their characters as representatives of everyday medieval humanity so that the members of the audience would be able to recognise themselves in the Shepherds and apply the message of Salvation which the Shepherds receive to themselves. There was no risk of contradicting the spare biblical narrative, which indeed stressed their representative qualities. A playwright could therefore experiment his craft much more freely with the Shepherds Play than in any of the other plays in the cycle. It is not surprising that this freedom led the Wakefield Master to create *two* Shepherds Plays with complex pre-Annunciation sequences, but this should not be seen merely as a result of his individual skills, for the Chester Cycle has a long Shepherds Play with quite as much non-biblical material, humour and dramatic effect. The Coventry Shepherds sequence is developed and divided into two in the Shearmen and Taylors' Pageant, with singing and feasting and even in the relatively undeveloped N-Town Shepherds Play there are clear signs of the basic Luke sequence having been augmented with inserts of singing. The Shepherds Plays invited elaboration and incorporation of material not strictly prescribed by the biblical narrative. None of the cycles presents a Shepherds Play which merely portrays the Annunciation by the Angel, the Journey to Bethlehem and the worship of the Christ-child.

The Shepherds in both *Secunda* and *Prima Pastorum* are fully-individualised characters who display traits of personality and social position which are recognisable to a medieval, and often to a modern, audience. Most remarkably, they do appear to be shepherds and show an exhaustive concern for their sheep and for the difficulties and techniques of sheep-keeping. Gyb in *Prima Pastorum* opens the play with a lament for his dead sheep which have been killed by 'the rott', the liver-fluke disease which was prevalent in Britain in the fourteenth and fifteenth centuries and which was responsible for killing hundreds of animals. His quarrel with II Shepherd about pasturing rights for as yet imaginary sheep (ll. 101–42) reflects the frequent disputes which arose between shepherds and between shepherds and farmers in the late four-teenth and early fifteenth centuries as more and more peasants turned to keeping sheep rather than tilling the fields, in order to take advantage of the higher economic gain to be achieved in this period at the height of Britain's prosperity as a wool and cloth producer. Wakefield itself was a town which had grown up and flourished with the wool trade and the shepherds' skills and problems displayed by the *Prima* and *Secunda Pastorum* Shepherds would have been especially relevant to Wakefield spectators, who would have been able to identify the Shepherds as people like themselves and thus ease the didactic function of the Shepherds

Play. Mak as a sheep thief played a role well known to the audience in real life where shepherds frequently suffered losses through theft.

In all the Shepherds Plays, the Shepherds complain and this serves to establish their identity as types of Common Man. The Wakefield Shepherds complain mostly about the conditions of their life rather than making the more generalised laments to be found in the other plays. Doctrinally the complaint is important for it demonstrates the disordered state of the world before the Birth of Christ, as do the quarrels and tricks which characterise the Wakefield Shepherds Plays before the appearance of the Angel, but the Wakefield Master seems to extend this motif yet further and use it as a means of exploiting the plays for social criticism. The complaints, particularly in *Prima Pastorum*, are concerned with abuses of power which the poorer classes have to suffer, taxes, the confiscation of their livestock or crops by officers of the lords or king, and the harsh treatment of servants by masters, all of which many members of the medieval audience may have experienced at first hand.

> Whoso says hym agane
> Were better be slane;
> Both ploghe and wane
> Amendys will not make.
>
> . . .
> We are so hammed,
> Fortaxed and rammed,
> We are made hand-tamed
> With these gentlery-men.
>
> . . .
> There shall come a swain as proud as a po;
> He must borrow my wain, my plough also;
>
> . . .
> He must have if he langed,
> If I should forgang it;
> I were better be hanged
> Then once say him nay.[6]

Some critics and social historians would see these episodes as proof of a singular revolutionary zeal in the Wakefield Master. While he may well have been wishing to draw attention to these conditions and invite those in a position to remedy them to do so through the implicit criticism within a Christmas play, it should be remembered that a convention of social complaint poetry using a rustic I-narrator existed in fifteenth-century literature, not least in *Piers Plowman* and subsequent imitations and continuations.[7] However, the complaints of *Secunda Pastorum* tend towards more conventional, stock and even humorous subjects such as shrewish wives and hen-pecked husbands (ll. 64–108) and this detracts a little from the Wakefield Master's force as a committed social critic. In many ways the complaints simply prepare the ground for Mak. Mak at his own word is a hen-pecked husband and when first seen by both the Shepherds and the audience puts on the airs of a proud Southerner, 'yeoman of the king' (ll. 201–7).

The III Shepherd's complaint in *Secunda Pastorum* details a world-out-of-joint with strange meteorological phenomena and visions added to the harsh conditions of his own life (ll. 117–44,154–71). The references to the cold weather would have been especially ironic with the Midsummer performance time of the Corpus Christi drama and it is quite possible that the episode was heightened for comic purpose with much non-verbal shivering, slapping of arms and chattering of teeth, although some critics feel that this particular sequence suggests a mystical or magical awareness of Evil stalking the world before the Birth of the Saviour.[8] The other two Shepherds' response is to quarrel with him at his pretensions to food and drink from them. He appears to be in their service rather than being an independent shepherd himself, as Iak Garcio is in *Prima Pastorum* and Trowle is in the Chester Shepherds Play. These three younger Shepherds are all sources of dispute in their plays, demonstrating lack of respect for the old from the young, the inversion of the master-servant relationship, and dis-ease in social relationships.

Disruption is also expressed in scenes of quarrelling and trickery and in the Shepherds Play is used structurally to contrast with the Post-Annunciation harmony of will and purpose when the Shepherds agree to go to Bethlehem, where they recognise and worship the god-head of the Christ-child. In *Prima Pastorum* I and II Shepherds quarrel over imaginary sheep and then over the distribution of beer in their feast and with Iak Garcio. The Chester Shepherds render their quarrel with Trowle physical in the wrestling match. In *Secunda Pastorum* the initial quarrel with III Shepherd is resolved and the extension of this disruptive element takes the form of the trick played on the Shepherds by Mak. Just as the trick I and II Shepherds play on III Shepherd in *Prima Pastorum* depends on things being not as they seem, the imaginary sheep which I and II *seem* to see, so Mak's trick relies on appearance and reality, for Mak has not been sleeping with the Shepherds when he says he has (l. 377 ff.) and the baby he shows them is by no means a real baby. In structural terms the Mak sequence is simply an extension of the quarrel and trick sequence present in *Prima Pastorum.*

Both *Prima Pastorum* and *Secunda Pastorum* follow the general Shepherds Play sequence of Shepherds' meeting – Shepherds' interaction – Annunciation of Angel – Journey to Bethlehem – Worship of Christ-child and presentation of gifts, and both provide the extended Meeting and Interaction sequence as a series of disruptions and attempted resolutions bounded by sleep and songs. The Wakefield Master makes effective use of the dramatic device of having his Shepherds being woken up by the angel for the Annunciation, while the other Shepherds Plays feature waking Shepherds throughout and this also successfully divides the extra, non-biblical material from the Post-Annunciation biblical sequence. The Mak episode play-within-a-play exploits this structure by corrupting the expected sequence when the Shepherds go to sleep. Instead of the Angel appearing to *bring* the message of Salvation, the birth of the Christ-child, the Lamb of God, Mak arises from sleep and starts a sequence of trickery and theft, *taking away* the real sheep which will later undergo a miraculous 'birth' according to Gill's ploy to hide the evidence. Once the trick has been discovered and the violent punishment of Mak has been affected (ll. 623–37), the Shepherds sleep again and this time the audience's expectations are confirmed for now the Angel does appear with the message of Salvation. Nothing more is heard of Mak and Gill, for they have no part in the true biblical sequence. In terms of staging, it is interesting to speculate that Mak and Gill were played by the same actors as Mary and Joseph, to emphasise the parody of Christ's birth represented by the disguise of the stolen sheep as a baby. In the same way, the wagon could have been used as Mak and Gill's house, with the Shepherds' scenes being played at ground level in front of the wagon, which then could have served as the Bethlehem stable, the site of the true miraculous birth.

The Mak story, without the Christmas Shepherds setting, exists in several versions in folk tale and while it is possible that many of these versions arose spontaneously in different locations, and thus possibly also in the Wakefield Master's imagination, it seems most likely that the *Secunda Pastorum* appearance of the theme is a conscious dramatisation of a tale known by playwright, audience and actors. The Wakefield Master's originality, if such it is, lies in having transformed the narrative material of the folk tale into dramatic form and grafted secular material onto the religious dramatic frame of the Corpus Christi plays. The Shepherds Play was a very suitable place to do this, as has already been seen, for it allowed space for the dramatist to develop both dramatic form and characters outside the bounds of biblical preconception and in addition the Shepherds, as rustic characters, had a strong link to the rural world and through this to folk lore and the folk drama. The Chester Shepherds Play similarly incorporates an element of the ritual folk drama, the Mummers' Plays, in the wrestling match between Trowle and his masters, especially in the challenges which are almost a direct quotation from the Mummers' Plays:

> False lad, fye on thy face!
> One this grownd thow shall have a fall.
>
> *Turkey Snipe* (Turkish Knight)
> Battle, battle, battle I will call,
> And see which on the ground shall fall.[9]

The Christmas season was also the period associated with Mummers' Plays and thus a Christmas Play might once again have created the associations in both author and audience's mind of the folk drama. No dramatic text for the Mak story has come down to us, apart from *Secunda Pastorum*, but it is not impossible that other dramatisations of it may have existed in popular drama performed by itinerant troupes of actors, for which the text has not survived. Only one text of such entertainment has survived, the thirteenth-century *Interludium de Clerico et Puella* which seems to have been a duet performance possibly also using a performing dog, and even this has unfortunately survived only in an incomplete form. It would be strange, however, if this piece represented a truly unique form and it seems very likely that many other secular, popular dramatic pieces for informal presentation existed in the medieval period but, due to the transitory nature of the form of popular entertainment, these have not survived in written form.[10]

Apart from the associations with shepherds of folk tale and of course the sheep which plays an essential role in the Mak story, the Wakefield Master was prompted to add this secular story to his Shepherds Play for the subtle parody of the Nativity which it can be shown to provide when placed in proximity to the events of Christ's Birth. Certainly these qualities of the tale are not discernible in the folk tale versions of the story and by his use of it within the Shepherds Play the Wakefield Master has added a new layer of understanding and effect to both the host play and the folk tale so that each underlines the themes and adds to the effect of the other. The parallels between the two parts of the play are numerous: what is stolen in the Mak play is a sheep, 'a fat wether have we lorn' (l. 451), while what is given in the traditional Shepherds Play is the Lamb of God, Christ; Mak is seen to be a false shepherd who harms the sheep while Christ will be the Good Shepherd who cares for his spiritual flock (John, X); Gill the shrewish wife is contrasted to the Virgin Mary, the obedient handmaiden of God; miraculous birth occurs in both Mak's cottage and in the Bethlehem stable; the sheep Mak steals is destined to satisfy Mak's bodily hunger, 'I would he were flain; I list well eat./ This twelvemonth was I not so fain of one sheep-meet' (ll. 323–4), while the birth and death of the Lamb of God will appease mankind's spiritual needs with the gift of Salvation.[11] The pure entertainment value of the Mak episode no doubt also proved attractive to author, actors and audience, though it is significant to note that in his use of popular or folk elements in *Secunda Pastorum* the Wakefield Master was careful to incorporate only material which did not contradict, but rather heightened, the doctrinal message of the play.

The Mak episode replaces the quarrel sequence in *Prima Pastorum* which features the irreverent irruption of Iak Garcio as a wild servant with no respect for the authority of his elders. In many ways Mak can also be linked to this disruptive figure who seems to come into the Shepherds Plays from the folk drama and

finds realisation also in Trowle, the unruly boy in the Chester
Shepherds Play. Folk drama, like Carnival, is imbued with the
theme of disrupting the established order and inverting values and
social roles for a permitted festival period of licence. Mak is a
disrupter of social order to a high degree. He is already a known
thief, one with no respect for property or ownership, when he first
appears:

> Is he come? Then ilkone take heed to his thing
> . . .
> And thou hast an ill noise
> Of stealing of sheep.
>
> (ll. 200, 224–5)

The subsequent theft and disguise of the sheep prove the truth of
his reputation and demonstrate also his untrustworthiness. Like
many Carnival characters, appearances and declarations are decep-
tive with Mak. At his first appearance he adopts a false social
identity as a yeoman of the king and then he claims that he is 'true
as steel' (l. 226) while his actions belie his words but introduce a
pun, evidence of the untrustworthiness of language itself: Mak's
true 'steel' becomes true *stealing* of sheep. His expansive claim to
be ready to eat the 'child' as proof of his honesty (l. 522) similarly
plays with seeming and reality. Mak also has more sinister
overtones as a disrupter which some critics have interpreted in
terms of his being intended as an Antichrist figure or the Devil.
Certainly the contrast with Christ seems intended, but his night-
spell at ll. 278–86 and the way Gill compares him to the Devil at
l. 407 ('Then may we see here the devil in a band') seem rather
to be pointers of his nonconformity to conventions rather than
doctrinal themes. Mak's disruptions of both society and the
Shepherds' world may seem to be concluded when he is punished
by the blanket-tossing, but the state of disorder he represents in
the larger context of the Shepherds Play can only reach resolution
with the coming of the Angel and the message of Salvation which
the Christ-child brings. As if to underline this end of the disorder
the Wakefield Master inserts the line previously used by Mak in
his deceit, now in relation to the promise of Salvation and the
final coming of truth and resolution:

It is true as steel
That prophets have spoken
(ll. 699–700)

When the Shepherds of *Secunda Pastorum* are awakened by the Angel's message they are not frightened by this supernatural event, as the Luke sequence indicates and as are the *Prima Pastorum* Shepherds, but immediately discuss the song of the Angel and attempt to imitate it. This is a theme found neither in the biblical narrative nor in other European medieval religious plays, but which appears in all the surviving English Shepherds Plays. It seems clear that this is a case of internal influence as the obvious insertion of this episode with interruption of characteristic speech order and new stanza form into the otherwise undeveloped N-Town Shepherds Play shows. The discussion of the Angel's song also appears in pictorial form in the Holkham Bible Picture Book where the Shepherds are shown imitating the Angel's song. It is impossible to ascertain in which of the plays this incident first appeared, but while in the other plays the imitation is used for comic effect as the Shepherds attempt, and fail, to reproduce the sounds of the Angel's Latin song 'Gloria in excelsis', in both the Wakefield Shepherds Plays the song is used as a further opportunity for developing the Shepherds' personalities and increasing their ease of identity as types of Common Man. Their discussion of the song is based on the music rather than the words and displays an advanced technical knowledge of musical terms:

Say, what was his song? Heard ye not how he cracked it,
Three breves to a long?
. . .
Was no crochet wrong, nor no thing that lacked it.
(ll. 656–8)

The imitation of the Angel's song is followed by another non-biblical element common to all the English Shepherds Plays, the discussion of prophecies of Christ's Birth. This is an incident which often jars modern critical expectations for it seems 'unrealistic' for the characters which have been created as examples of medieval true-life shepherds suddenly to be given learned prophecies to expound and interpret. It is important to remember that realism as a concept in drama is a recent development and this use of the Shepherds would not have seemed so inconsistent to a medieval audience. Within the overall structure of the Corpus Christi cycle, the Shepherds Play lies at the point of balance between the pre-Salvation and the Salvation world. Only once the Angel's message has been given to the Shepherds does mankind know that there is the possibility of Salvation rather than the inevitable clutches of the Devil which followed from Adam's choice in the Garden of Eden. The promise of Salvation which the Old Testament prophets had referred to again and again has now been fulfilled. It is important for the progress of the cycle therefore to emphasise this linking role of the Shepherds Play and to demonstrate the relevance of the Old Testament promises and typology to the New Testament and so to the Christian and contemporary medieval world. The medieval drama never abandoned the doctrinal or didactic motivation of the plays in favour of humour or entertainment, and just as the Wakefield Master incorporated an effective piece of secular entertainment into his Shepherds Play where it was appropriate and useful to the official material of the play with the Mak episode, so here he retains the traditional role of the Shepherds as mouthpieces of the prophecies of Christ. He does, however, keep his Shepherds' characters fully in evidence as they still interrupt one another, and in *Prima Pastorum* make good-natured fun of each other as they discuss the prophecies.

Once the Shepherds have discussed the meaning of the Angel's song and related it to prophecies of the Saviour's Birth, they set off on the journey to Bethlehem to find and worship the Christ-child. In terms of the staging of the plays it is possible that this journey is very short in terms of distance covered as the Shepherds move representationally from 'the fields' where they have been watching the sheep and sleeping to the Bethlehem stable. In all likelihood the fields were the space in front of the wagon and the stable the wagon stage itself. With the rudimentary scenery and props of medieval drama often the location intended for a scene is indicated purely by the presence of certain characters in it, or by direct statement in the dialogue. Thus the appearance of Mary, Joseph and the Christ-child on the wagon would be enough to set the wagon as the Bethlehem stable. If the wagon had previously represented Mak and Gill's house the change of characters on it would be all that was required for a medieval audience to accept it as the new Bethlehem location. The Shepherds follow the star to Bethlehem, possibly a star attached to a pole and carried by an 'extra' or possibly a star on a pulley system like that used in the York Last Judgement Play. The star would have been produced using a torch or candles and it is interesting to note that the York Shepherds Play was produced by the Chandlers', or Candlemakers, Guild which would have been able to provide the means for producing an impressive light show while demonstrating their own wares to the audience.

The Luke sequence makes no mention of the star appearing to the Shepherds but medieval narrative and dramatic tradition adopted it, probably in analogy with the star which appeared to the Magi. In exactly the same way the Shepherds were generally believed to have presented gifts to the Christ-child, just as the Magi presented their gold, frankincense and myrrh as related in Matthew. Each Shepherds Play has its own version of the gifts which the Shepherds offer but these are always much more humble than those of the Magi, representing the kind of items that real-life shepherds might have been likely to have given as gifts. However, the Wakefield Master in his plays seems to make the gifts work on the symbolic level of the Magi's gifts too, combining both realism and allegorical intention. The cherries, bird and ball which the *Secunda Pastorum* Shepherds give to the Christ-child can be interpreted as symbols of the dual nature of humanity and divinity which resides uniquely in the Saviour.[12]

The Virgin Mary closes both the Wakefield Shepherds Plays by granting God's blessing to the Shepherds and instructing them to broadcast the news of the Birth to all they meet. It is at this point that the Nativity Shepherds' other representative role is displayed, as priests, the interpreters of God's will to mankind. Pastoral imagery for priests had already a strong tradition in the Christian religion by the medieval period and indeed holds still today when 'Pastor' (shepherd) is used as a religious title and the faithful are referred to as 'the flock'. The Shepherds as Priests role had been prepared for by the discussion of the prophecies and by the close of the play, as the Shepherds exit singing, the double function of Shepherds as representative humble Common Men to whom the promise of Salvation is first made and representatives of the spiritual guides for those who follow the new faith which the birth of Christ heralds is firmly established. The Wakefield Master concludes his plays with the didactic message of the Shepherds Play in a tone of adoration and dignity which contrasts with the earlier roughness of the Shepherds' interaction but which by no means contradicts it. Like all medieval Corpus Christi cycle drama, the religious significance of the plays is not sacrificed to secular humour or dramatic development, but the one is used to establish and emphasise the other.

4
York 'Crucifixion Play'

A wealth of details in civic documents, guild accounts and church records survives for the organisation and performance of the York Mystery Cycle and the text survives complete in one manuscript which clearly indicates its provenance from York. Although this material gives many indications as to the method of staging the plays and to the status the cycle had in the life of the city, it does offer certain contradictions and is still far from providing a clear, full picture of the presentation of the cycle. The role of the trade guilds is quite clear and both civic records and the manuscript show the assignation of the individual plays to particular guilds.

The York material also records the method of financing the plays through 'pageant silver' collected from each member of the guild and augmented by contributions from fines for shoddy work or breaking guild rules. Each guild appointed a 'pageant master' who was responsible each year for the preparation of the play and who organised repairs to the pageant wagon, costumes, the purchase of items necessary for the performance, selection of actors and holding of rehearsals. A document surviving from the accounts of the York Mercers' guild, which produced the spectacular Last Judgement Play, shows that wagons could be highly decorated and contain machinery for an actor playing God, or an icon of God, to be raised and lowered from the floor of the wagon playing space.[1] Maintenance of and responsibility for the wagon was therefore a demanding job for the pageant master.

All the details in the York records point to a 'true processional'

manner of performance whereby the individual pageant wagons
of each craft guild on which the plays were performed gathered at
the Gates of Holy Trinity Church, Micklegate, at 4.30 a.m. on
Corpus Christi Day and were then drawn to a number of sites, or
'stations', in the city where they stopped and performed their play,
ending up outside the Church of All Saints, Pavement. (See the
map of York pageant stations by Meg Twycross, on p. 63.) Despite
these details some critics have felt that such a method of staging
is not practically possible, for the time required to perform
sequentially the 52 pageants of the York Cycle at the ten to sixteen
stations which are indicated in various years would far exceed a
dawn-to-midnight playing period on Corpus Christi Day. Others
have felt that even if this were the case for York, there is no
reason to assume that this was the method of staging the cycle
plays in other cities. Until we discover a full eye-witness account
of the Corpus Christi plays in performance, clearly dated and
referring to a named city, this kind of debate can never firmly be
closed, but for York at least it seems reasonable to respect the
records we do have and accept the 'true-processional' mode of
staging for the York Cycle.[2]

A record relating to the Crucifixion Play gives support to the
theory that all the plays were performed at all the stations. In 1422
representatives of the Guild of the Painters and Stainers and the
Guild of the Pinners and Latteners (workers with brass or similar
metals) went before the Mayor and Council to propose an
amalgamation of their two pageants as 'the play on the day of
Corpus Christi . . . is impeded more than usual because of the
multitude of pageants . . . knowing that the matter of both
pageants could be shown together in one pageant for the shortening
of the play rather profitably . . .'.[3] It was decided that the Painters'
and Stainers' pageant 'should be . . . removed' and that the
Pinners' and Latteners' pageant be maintained with the addition
of 'the speeches which were previously performed . . . in the
pageant of the Painters and Stainers'.[4] Both guilds were to be
responsible for the financing of the new combined play. The
stretching and nailing of Christ on the Cross, which had previously
been the responsibility of the Painters and Stainers, was added to
the raising up of the Crucified [Christ] on the Mount, which had
been the responsibility of the Pinners' and Latteners' Guild, to
produce the play which has survived in the manuscript of the York

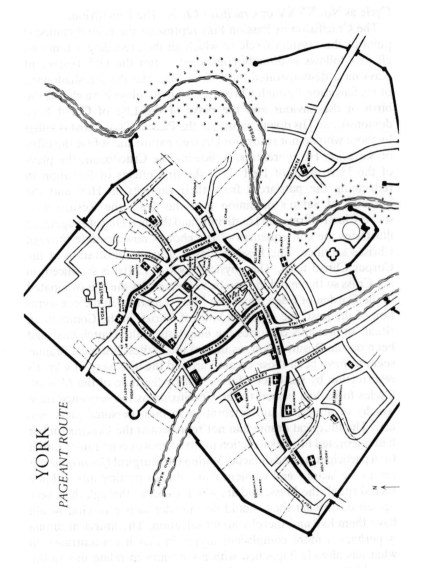

YORK
PAGEANT ROUTE

Cycle as No. XXXV or *Crucifixio Christ*, The Crucifixion.

The Crucifixion or Passion Play represents the central climactic point of the Mystery Cycle to which all the preceding action and all that follows is directly connected. After the Old Testament plays have demonstrated the Fall of Man and the foreshadowing of his Salvation through Christ, the Nativity plays have shown the birth of the Saviour and the plays of the Life of Christ have demonstrated His divine nature, in the Passion Play Christ is killed by those who do not recognise His true nature and refuse the offer of Salvation He represents. Following the Crucifixion, the plays of the Harrowing of Hell show the first effects of Salvation in redeeming the patriarchs from their captivity in Hell and the breaking of Satan's dominion over the dead, the Resurrection shows Christ affirmed in His divinity and the final Day of Judgement illustrates the consequences of the choices now possible through Christ's sacrifice. The Passion Play is also the illustration of the Corpus Christi feast. The physical body of Christ is sacrificed on the Cross so that mankind can be redeemed for the sins originated in the Garden of Eden which the Mass celebrates in the consecration of the host, the symbolic body of Christ, in the Communion ritual. In previous centuries the emphasis in the church year had been on the Resurrection, as indeed the earliest liturgical dramas seem to have been those created around the discovery of Christ's resurrection by the three Maries, but by the time of the Mystery Cycles focus had passed to the Crucifixion as the sequence most worthy of attention and celebration in both personal piety and art.[5] The liturgical drama had not represented the Crucifixion but had celebrated the Resurrection for its focus was celebratory rather than participatory and didactic. Within the liturgical *Quem quaeritis* pieces the 'actors' and 'audience' are already participants within a sacred ritual, the Mass, and are already aware, through their very presence, of what they should do in order to live as God would have them live and thereby attain salvation. The liturgical drama is perhaps a more complacent drama in that it concentrates on what has already happened with no attempt to relate this to the actual lives of those present. In contrast, the Mystery Cycle plays focus on the present, showing the past of the biblical events to be integrally connected both to the present of the audience and actors and also to their future in terms of salvation or damnation. The cycle plays work within 'God's time' which is universal and contemporaneous, fixing the individual within the flow of Christian history.[6] They are an active, didactic drama.

In order to appreciate the importance of Christ's sacrifice, which occurred in a past specific time and place, to appreciate the possibility of salvation which it offered to Christians of all times and places and to apprehend its relevance, late medieval theology and practical religion recommended the intense concentration on and contemplation of the Passion of Christ. Franciscan theology in particular exhorted the consideration of the practical details of the Crucifixion and Christ's suffering as a means of understanding the immense gift which the Sacrifice offered to mankind. The preaching of the Franciscan friars, who travelled extensively throughout the country giving sermons in churches or wherever a crowd might be gathered, was an important means of spreading this idea to all levels of the general populace. Works written for the private consumption of the more highly educated and pious such as the various versions of the *Meditationes Vitae Christi*, translated into English by Nicholas Love as the *Mirrour of the Blessyd Lyf of Jesu Christ* (1410), explicitly recommended the contemplation of the minute details of the Crucifixion as a meditation aid to understanding the nature of Christ's sacrifice and to appreciate the potential of Salvation which it represented:

> who soo desyreth with thappostle Poule to be Joyeful in the crosse of oure lorde ihesu crist / and in the blessid passion / he must with hely meditacion theryn for the grete mysteryes & al the processe therof yf they were inwardly consyderyd with alle the inward mynde and beholdyng of mannes soule / as I fully trowe they shold brynge that beholder in to a newe state of grace. For to hym that wold serche the passion of oure lorde with all his herte and all his inward affection there sholde come many deuoute felynges and sterynges that he neuer supposed before.[7]

To a certain extent this interest in consideration of details was part of the general intellectual climate in the fourteenth and fifteenth centuries. The nominalist philosophers at Oxford in the early fourteenth century had introduced the idea of the importance of details in defining the individuality of things and of experience of these details as being the key to reality. Something could be understood through direct personal experience of it. The same focus on and exploration of details can be seen in the visual arts of the fifteenth century as attention moved from the earlier exclusive concentration on the symbolic, iconographical element or action which is characteristic of Romanesque art. In fifteenth century art, and in the drama, the symbolic action does not disappear, but is surrounded by a greater display of contextualising place; it no longer takes place in an abstract, symbolic environment, but in perceptually visible and identifiable surroundings.[8] Detail is not added merely for decorative effect, but in order to relate the event it portrays to the life of those who look at the picture. In the same way, the cycle plays illustrate the events of Christian history with the details of character, dialogue, humour, pomp and cruelty which can relate them more immediately to the lives of the spectators. The portrayal is more immediate for drama enables the enactment of sequences of events, showing cause and effect and progression, which pictorial representation cannot achieve so effectively. The involvement of the individual spectators is more intense and effective as the characters speak directly to them.[9]

The Passion Play is the moment of the cycle which most directly affects the audience and which doctrinally most requires audience-involvement. The spectators must experience the sacrifice of Christ to understand its relevance but they must also be made aware of how they too are involved in the killing of Christ as representatives of Fallen Man whom He died to save. This twofold experience and recognition is achieved in the Mystery Cycle Passion Plays through extensive use of brutal physical detail and the use of executioners, torturers or simple soldiers who are ordered to carry out the Crucifixion by their leaders. In the York Crucifixion Play the religious and political authorities are entirely absent and the only characters are Christ and four soldiers who go about the practical business of performing the Crucifixion. The use of these four 'rude mechanicals' achieves both the doctrinal points of the play: the details of their work stress the suffering of Christ and their interest in their work, their banter and their blatant unawareness of any kind of moral responsibility for what they are doing establishes the implication and guilt of Common Man in the Crucifixion.

The four soldiers go about the Crucifixion purely in terms of a job that has to be done. They are unnamed, like almost all of the non-biblical characters in the cycle plays, standing as representatives of Common Man who follows his orders and does his job without worrying about any higher moral responsibility or indeed the moral consequences of what he is doing. For them, crucifying Christ is merely a problem of stretching and nailing which they affront with hammers, nails and ropes and any unwillingness to perform it or doubts that they might have stem exclusively from the amount of effort involved or the fact that the equipment they have to work with has been badly prepared. Their concerns are all physical and practical, with no spiritual or moral overtones and this is already an indication of their status in the moral framework of the Mystery plays. Like Cain, they perceive the physical rather than the spiritual import of what they do; like Fallen Man, they cannot recognise the spiritual universe represented by the possibility of grace. When they attempt to fix Christ's hands to the cross they discover that the nail-holes are badly placed and too widely spaced to accommodate His arms. The same problem occurs when they attempt to fix His feet, for the hole has been made too low down on the Cross (ll. 107–12, 126–7). 4 soldier remarks that the 'work is all unmeet', but he is referring only to the bad workmanship they are being confronted with and must attempt to adapt in order to perform an efficient crucifixion, not to any moral qualms about the justice or cruelty of the Crucifixion of Christ. It is left to the spectators, the potentially saved, to grasp the extra, spiritual, meaning to his words.

When the soldiers have managed to nail Christ to the Cross, having overcome the practical problems of the wrongly-spaced holes by the cunning use of ropes to stretch His limbs longer to meet the holes (ll. 113–14, 129–40) they next have to confront the task of raising the Cross, with the crucified Christ on it, so that it stands on 'yon hill' as they have been instructed. They are less than enthusiastic at the prospect of such heavy work and once they have begun (l. 186), they begin to make loud complaints at how much they are suffering under the weight:

> For-great harm have I hent:
> My shoulder is asunder.
> . . .
> This cross and I in two must twin,
> Else breaks my back asunder soon.
> (ll. 189–94)

There is no concern expressed for the suffering of Christ which is obviously many times greater, the soldiers are interested only in the pain that they feel, in the physical effects of their work, not in the spiritual implications of what they are doing. Of course, to the members of the audience watching the play the contrast in suffering is very apparent, and the attention given by the soldiers to their petty suffering underlines all the more the enormity of Christ's physical suffering as well as the spiritual implications of this which are evident to the privileged point of view of the audience. Once again the soldiers can only perceive how their work affects them materially, while the audience can appreciate the effects that this 'job' will have on the spiritual destiny not only of the four soldiers but of all mankind. When the soldiers complain of aching backs the audience can identify on a personal level, remembering that in performing similar tasks of lifting or stretching they too have suffered such aches or pains, or would suffer them and no doubt similarly voice their pain. In this way, Christ's silence is all the more dramatic and revealing. He who suffers infinitely more is silent while those who cause him the pain make loud moans and groans. Christ's silence is a motif which appears in all the plays of the Passion sequence, from the Arrest in the Garden of Gethsemane through the Trials and Buffetings, and is indeed attested to in the scriptural narrative. Christ makes no answer to his accusers either to deny their claims or to attempt to save Himself. The contrast here between the response to pain of the four soldiers and Christ, particularly with respect to the amount of pain and proportional response, is perhaps the most moving and effective dramatic use of this silence.

Throughout their work, the soldiers treat Christ merely as another piece of their equipment, as an object rather than a person and certainly not as a God. Once the job is done and the Cross finally fixed securely with wedges so that it remains upright without wobbling (ll. 229–48), the soldiers can relax a little and turn to Christ to ask Him, mockingly, what He thinks of their handiwork. Once again the irony is there for the more informed and perceptive spectator who can understand the larger meaning of the 'work' they have 'wrought' and it is to the audience, rather than to the soldiers, that Christ replies. His answer is concerned with the wider issues of their 'work' and calls on 'All men that walk by way or street' to contemplate the soldiers' handiwork and to think

about it carefully, just as the friars and the writers of the
Meditationes Vitae Christi invited the pious to feel experientially
the details of the Crucifixion and the pain that Christ must have
experienced.

> All men that walk by way or street,
> Take tent ye shall no travail tine;
> Behold my head, my hands, my feet,
> And fully feel now, ere ye fine,
> If any mourning may be meet,
> Or mischief measured unto mine.
>   (ll. 253–8)

In the context of the staging of the pageants, of course, the men
that walk by the way or street are the spectators themselves,
gathered around the pageant wagon in the streets of York. Christ
then asks for forgiveness, in the play time for the soldiers who
have nailed Him to the Cross, but in God's time for all mankind,
including the audience, and for salvation:

> Therefore, my Father, I crave,
> Let never their sins be sought,
> But see their souls to save.
>   (ll. 262–4)

The involvement of the audience now passes from direct identification with the soldiers to a sequence of suspense and hope
engendered and inevitably denied by foreknowledge of the story.
The soldiers remain unaware of what they are caught up in even
after Christ's speech, and their response demonstrates yet again
their lack of recognition both of who Christ is and what He
represents. The audience is necessarily struck by this refusal to
appreciate what is happening, for from their privileged position in
God's time they understand the implication. The soldiers begin to
associate Christ with rumours they have heard of someone who
claimed to be God's son and said he would destroy the Temple
(l. 273). This offers a tantalising hope to the audience that
recognition is imminent, but once again the soldiers are capable
of perceiving only the physical and not the spiritual, for they reject
such claims stating that Christ had neither enough physical strength

nor sufficient followers to knock the Temple down and build it up
again. It is the audience who understands the metaphorical,
spiritual meaning. The soldiers' last words on the matter are that
they have done as Pilate ordered them to do, a final refusal to
accept any kind of responsibility for what they have done.

Like the Shepherds as ordinary representatives of Common Man
to whom the possibility of salvation is first offered, the soldiers or
torturers are representatives of ordinary working men who refuse
to recognise and accept this possibility. They can be seen as the
negative image of the Shepherds and are just as important to the
doctrinal technique of the cycle plays. Each individual Christian
is responsible for his or her own destiny in making the decision
whether or not to accept the possibility of salvation which Christ's
sacrifice represents. The Shepherds accept, the soldiers do not.
The Shepherds recognised the Christ-child as the Son of God and
worshipped Him, the soldiers refuse to consider His God-head
and nail Him to the Cross. These are in essence the two choices
available to individual Christians and the cycle plays offer portray-
als of these two groups of characters which will ease the identification of the audience with them and thus help them to see that the
choice is relevant to their lives too.

The dramatic expression of the Crucifixion as a job of work and
the practical exponents of it as ordinary working men assure
audience identification. The medieval trade and craftsmen watching the play could apply details of the work and problems of
adapting awkward materials to their own life and work. Many in
the medieval audience and indeed today could recognise the
concern only with the present moment of their work and the
refusal to think about what would happen to their work, or the
stage in a long piece of work for which they were responsible,
once it left their hands. Responsibility is often deferred to those
higher in the labour hierarchy whose task it is to plan, judge and
consider consequences. The four York soldiers are quite clear
about the requirements of their job and their position in the order
of authority. When 1 Soldier begins to get authoritarian and tell
the others what to do they are quick to resent such a presumption:
'Yea, thou commandest lightly as a lord;/Come help to hale him,
with ill hail!' (ll. 115–16).

Although the soldiers are not given individual names they are
by no means types or abstractions. Their dialogue is recognisably

realistic and personalities can be seen through their responses. 1 Soldier appears to be the foreman of the gang, or at least takes on this role. He orders the work to start, tells the others what to do, asks how they are getting on and suggests solutions to the technical problems they encounter. He also noticeably does less hard work than the others, choosing the head of the Cross to hold (ll. 87–8) and later preferring to order rather than help haul (ll. 117–18). 4 Soldier is the most conscientious and it is he who notices the defects in their equipment and who then wishes to report the job done to their superiors as soon as they have attached Christ to the Cross (ll. 151–2).

Staging requirements seem to have influenced the number of soldiers in the York play. There are four soldiers in the play rather than the standard grouping of three used in both scriptural narrative and other plays presumably because a minimum of four men were required to raise the Cross, one at the head, one at the foot and one each side. The actors in the play lift the Cross upright from the ground where it lies as they attach Christ to it to slot it into a mortice which holds it firmly for all to see. The mechanics of this elevation must have been carefully worked out and its execution represented a testimony to the skill of the actors and their guild just as it did within the play time to the four soldiers carrying out their commission from Pilate. The play itself has no stage directions and the sequence of actions and techniques involved must be drawn out from the dialogue.[10] No list of props or details of the wagon used survive in the records of the Pinners' and Painters' Guild, but from the text the minimum properties appear to be a wooden cross, hammers, nails, a mortice, wedges, ropes and for the final section of the play where the soldiers squabble over Christ's clothes, a coat.

The soldiers refer several times to a hill on which they are supposed to mount the Cross and the 1415 description of the play in the general plays list refers to the raising of the Cross 'upon the mount of Calvary'.[11] The stretching and nailing section of the play must surely have taken place on the wagon itself so that it would be clearly visible to the spectators, rather than on the ground in front of the wagon. The elevation of the Cross could also be played here and the slipping of it into a mortice fixed onto the wagon floor. Unless the Pinners and Painters had two wagons, one of which was smaller, like the Mercers' second Hell-mouth wagon, and represented Mount Calvary, it is difficult to imagine how the hill references in the dialogue could be realised in practical staging terms. It is unlikely that all the dialogue with reference to carrying the Cross to 'yon hill' and the lengthy complaints about how heavy it is would be inappropriate to the action. Because of this it seems likely that the sequence from lines 211 to 218 could cover carrying the Cross either onto the wagon from the ground or down from the wagon and onto a secondary wagon representing the mount. Lines 219 to 225 could then represent the final upright elevation of the Cross and the sliding of it into 'this mortice here' (l. 220). The iconographical importance of Christ on the Cross seems to require that this final image be well visible, on an elevated place, to the whole audience.

The fixing of Christ to the Cross on the ground, or 'supine Crucifixion' was already a common iconographical and narrative feature and many visual representations of the Passion also show ropes being used to stretch Christ's limbs and the holes in the cross being obviously too widely spaced. The technique is also featured in the Cornish Cycle Passion Play and it is interesting to note that the Chester Passion Play was performed by the Guild of the Ironmongers and Ropers. It is difficult to say whether drama drew its inspiration here from the narrative or visual tradition or vice versa, but the use of ropes was certainly necessary in the cycle plays in order to attach the actor playing Christ firmly to the Cross. The stretching motif may have been introduced in order to give a motivation for the necessary introduction of these ropes. Although the actor playing Christ no doubt did suffer physical discomfort, it is clear that actual nails were not used to fix his body to the Cross in performance. The image of the Crucifixion was extremely diffuse in fourteenth- and fifteenth-century religious art, yet the physical demonstration of the fixing, elevation and hanging of a live actor representing Christ must have been a much more effective and emotionally striking portrayal than that offered in the visual arts. The associated immediacy for the audience of witnessing the Crucifixion in the familiar surroundings of their own town, played out by people they knew socially or commercially is not to be underestimated in the creation of strong religious feeling and as exhortation to repentance and God-fearing life.

The use of realistic details in order to evoke emotional apprehension is used in all the plays of the York Passion sequence and indeed in many other of the Mystery Cycle plays, but only in the Crucifixion Play is it used primarily to create identification between the members of the audience and the physical perpetrators of the killing of Christ. In the other plays of the York sequence the details are not so clearly physical but rather psychological and this has led critics to identify them as the work of one author, now generally known as the York Realist. This playwright was careful to add details which motivated or explained decisions or actions and followed through 'processes of behaviour' so that the events became comprehensible to the audience in terms of individual characters doing certain things for reasons stemming from their lives and situations rather than merely because they were part of a preordained symbolic sequence.[12] The Crucifixion Play is not generally considered to form part of the canon of the York Realist, despite Cawley's affirmation in the introduction to his edition of the play, and in this play the realistic details are physical rather than psychological and are used both to heighten the emotional effect of the Crucifixion and to force an awareness of direct identification with the soldiers and thereby an implicit involvement in the responsibility for Christ's sacrifice.

Mankind's responsibility for the Crucifixion comes about because the Fallen world to which we belong is the result of Adam and Eve's original sin. In this sense the Crucifixion is a necessary corollary to the Fall of Man and as mankind sinned once in the Garden of Eden, so mankind will sin again in killing the Redeemer. The significant difference this time is that there will now be a possible happy outcome for those who choose to recognise Christ's sacrifice. Following the Fall, even the good souls were trapped in Hell from whence Christ liberates them after the Crucifixion in the Harrowing of Hell. Paradoxically, if Christ had not been crucified then mankind could not have been saved, but the Crucifixion was a result of mankind's choice, not of God's predetermination, a choice was made not to recognise good but to follow evil just as Adam had the choice not to follow the evil of the serpent's offer of the apple and disobedience in Eden. In Christ's first speech in the Crucifixion Play, he points to the inevitable link between His sacrifice and Adam's sin (ll. 49–60). He does not plead to be spared the pain of the Crucifixion but for His suffering to gain defence for mankind from evil:

That they for me may favour find;
And from the fiend them fend,
So that their souls be safe
In wealth withouten end.

(ll. 56–9)

The York Passion sequence clearly demonstrates that the responsibility for the Crucifixion is mankind's and not Satan's, though the Chester sequence suggests that Satan was principally to blame. The Dream of Pilate's Wife incident which is included in Play XXX, *Christ before Pilate I*, in the York sequence exculpates Satan by showing how he tries to stop the Crucifixion by sending a warning dream to Pilate's wife, not from any good will to mankind, but because he realises that once Christ is killed mankind will no longer be under his dominion.

The chattering of the soldiers and their interest in their work not only enables the members of the audience to see themselves in them and so establish their own role in the Christian story, but it also serves as a means of demonstrating the divinity of Christ. The soldiers are noisy and brutal, their physical violence towards Christ is matched by a violence of language in their swearing by Mahomet (ll. 61, 129), their jeering and their quarrelling. They are full of energy and as they bustle around attempting to finish their job they represent Common Man at his most vital yet least refined. They are fixed on the physical level and cannot comprehend moral responsibility or spiritual meaning. The overwhelming contrast between their noise and energy and Christ's silence and passivity is striking even in a reading of the play and in performance it would have been even greater. Christ does not talk to the soldiers even when they directly address Him but talks only to God and to mankind in general as represented by the audience. He is cooperative, yet passive; He lies down on the Cross when ordered to do so and makes no complaint as the soldiers stretch His limbs with the ropes, nail His hands and feet and then jar Him violently as the Cross is dropped into the mortice: 'This falling was more fell/Than all the harms he had;' (ll. 225–6). Christ is not what the soldiers are, Fallen Man in unbridled, ungoverned state, His dignity and silence before their rowdy brutality establishes this, yet He is Man, He has chosen to be born as a Man and to be killed for mankind's sake. The delight the soldiers seem to take in detailing the pain they are causing Him underlines Christ's physical nature. His sinews can snap when stretched, and do, His veins can burst as no doubt a sachet of paint provided by the Painters was burst to demonstrate at line 147, yet He makes no complaint. The soldiers, able to perceive only at the physical level, interpret this as a demonstration of His lack of God-head, for surely a divinity would be immune from such pain (ll. 187–8), yet, as is apparent to the audience, this is in fact a proof of His divinity and the payment He has agreed to make for Adam and Fallen Man's sins.

In the other plays of the Passion sequence Christ is contrasted with His accusers and tormentors in order to establish what he is by demonstrating the falsity of what they think He is. He is contrasted with the worldly king, Herod, who rages and struts and establishes His own nature as Heavenly King. He remains silent in front of Annas and Caiphas' accusations that he has broken their law, the Old Judaic Law, for He is a representative of the New Law, the Christian Law. The torturers in the Buffeting and Scourging plays attempt to humiliate Christ through mockery and physical abuse, yet only underline His dignity as their cruel games have no effect. The doctrinal lesson of Christ's nature as God and Man is demonstrated through the treatment He receives from contrasting types of human civic and religious authority and Common Man. York has no Buffeting Play, as do the Towneley-Wakefield and Chester and, according to stage directions, the N-Town, Cycles, in which Christ is flogged and beaten by torturers, and their role is taken by the soldiers of the Crucifixion Play. Whereas the torturers of the Wakefield *Coliphizacio* delight in their 'game' of harming Christ, the York soldiers simply show no concern for how their work, the nailing and raising, may harm Christ. In this way they are perhaps shown as being less culpable for it is not their will to harm Christ, they simply make no efforts to spare Him pain. Indeed the transference of the 'Father forgive them, for they know not what they do' plea from Christ which in Luke comes when Christ is on the Cross, with a general application, to during the nailing directs an idea of forgiveness to these representatives of Common Man themselves which is not present in the other cycles. Christ's compassion is underlined by the positioning of this plea as much as it is demonstrated by contrast with the soldiers who have none towards Him.[13]

The Chester Cycle includes the Crucifixion in a longer play which passes from the Road to Calvary, the nailing and elevation, Christ on the Cross, Longinus to the Deposition with Nichodemus. In this play the required establishment of audience identification with characters involved in the Crucifixion is anticipated through an episode with four Jews, possibly soldiers working for Caiphas or Pilate, who quarrel over and eventually dice for Christ's clothes before the Crucifixion actually takes place. Their role as Common Man is illustrated through their quarrelling, their banter and the dice-game itself before Caiphas loses patience with them and tells them to get on with the Crucifixion. This is a much longer version of the episode which is tagged on to the end of the York Crucifixion Play in the position suggested in the Gospels and also followed in the N-Town and Towneley-Wakefield plays. Whereas the York soldiers draw lots for the clothes, after an initial quarrel, as in the Gospel version, the Chester, Towneley-Wakefield and N-Town soldiers dice for them as a method of distribution which is much more entertaining for the audience and can recall their own experiences of gambling. The stretching and nailing in the Chester play is not as extended as in the York play though once again the problem of the holes being drilled in the wrong place and the need for stretching with ropes is used. The Chester workmen are not as involved in their work as their York counterparts, for the didactic point of identification has already been established by the dice-game and a longer sequence here is not necessary. The result is in fact a much less moving play, for the Crucifixion itself becomes one of a series of incidents which follow one another and so loses in majesty.

The Towneley-Wakefield and N-Town Cycles also make the Crucifixion part of a longer sequence concluding with the material covered in the York Mortificacio Play, No. XXXVI. Towneley-Wakefield uses the four torturers of the Buffeting Play as the four workmen required to attach Christ to the Cross and set it up and they carry with them from the earlier play the spirit of game and mock. Their labour in the stretching, nailing and elevation becomes a continuation of the game and their brutality is fully aware and directed rather than the more incidental, though none the less callous, concentration on work of the York soldiers. When Christ asks God for forgiveness, for they know not what they do, the torturers roundly reply that they know quite well what they are doing and their guilt becomes conscious intent rather than lack of perception of the spiritual level above the physical level. The tournament imagery used in their game in the Buffeting Play is carried over as they set Christ onto His 'palfrey', the Cross, and despite their energy and boisterousness they are louts having fun rather than workmen refusing to see the consequences of their labour.

The Towneley-Wakefield Christ makes a lengthy lament from the Cross in which attention is called to His suffering as the price which must be paid for Adam's sin, the 'ransom' required to redeem mankind. There is a similar sequence in the N-Town Play which is answered by a lament from the Virgin who in this play almost steals the attention from Christ. The Gospel account of Christ asking John to take care of His mother is elaborated to produce a melodramatic series of swoons, weeping and laments with the Virgin clinging to the Cross and refusing to be led away.

All the Crucifixion Plays in the Mystery Cycles, both the compact York play and the more extended sequences in the other cycles, make extensive use of the image of seeing and understanding. The Mystery Cycles themselves are bound up in this dichotomy for the physical events they show are to be interpreted in a larger sense than is apparent to the characters within them. The audience is constantly being asked to see and to make the leap from sensory perception to intellectual understanding. The soldiers and torturers apprehend only what they see, a man having made fanciful claims who is to be punished, a man who has no material attributes of a king and thus he cannot be a king, a man who is physically weak and who therefore cannot throw down the Temple. The audience in contrast sees the actions and apprehends the moral and religious significance within both the Christian story and their own personal destiny. When the N-Town Jew tells his colleagues to set up the Cross, with Christ on it, so 'þat we may loke hym in þe face' (l. 759), it is obvious to the audience that though the Jews will look at the image they will not understand what it implies, for they are blind to the spiritual significance. The apocryphal legend of Longinus, a blind man who was goaded into spearing Christ's side by those who had crucified Him, was used to emphasise this spiritual blindness. When the blood from the wound flows onto Longinus' face he is miraculously cured of his blindness and sees not only what he has done, wounded Christ, but what Christ is, and comprehends at once His divinity. He craves forgiveness for he knew not what he did and the words consciously echo Christ's plea to God for forgiveness. Christ's torturers and their superiors are by analogy morally blind, but the audience, like the miraculously cured Longinus, can both see and understand the significance of the Crucifixion. Adam's sin had been prompted by a desire to know Good from Evil and now with Christ's sacrifice the desire has been finally achieved for those who recognise Christ and Good will be saved.[14]

5
Chester 'Last Judgement Play'

From the text of the plays and the details of organisation and performance which remain in civic and trade records, the Chester Cycle seems to have developed, flourished and continued later than the other three surviving complete cycles. Whereas York and Towneley-Wakefield have clear documentary evidence to support a developed cycle and staging in the fifteenth century, Chester details come mainly from the sixteenth century.[1] From the few details which can be gleaned from fifteenth-century records it would appear that up until *c.* 1519–20 Chester had a play performed after the Corpus Christi Procession, produced by various guilds of the city in one place, in front of St John's Church at the end of the procession route. The play was possibly only a Passion Play and not a complete cycle. As rents for pageant houses are recorded during the fifteenth century, it would appear that the plays were staged on wagons. After 1519–20, the term used to describe the plays changes from 'Corpus Christi Play' to 'the Whitsun plays' and remains as this until the last recorded performance in 1575. It would seem that once the plays were removed from Corpus Christi Day to the Whitsun period they underwent considerable elaboration and development to spread to a complete cycle performed processionally on wagons by the trade guilds over a three-day period.

The city of Chester already had an important Midsummer Fair which was held at Whitsuntide and a traditional ceremonial licensing of the Minstrels. There would have been both the existing

79

expectations of holiday atmosphere and entertainment and a chance to increase the flux of people who came into the city in this period and thereby increase the volume of trade to motivate the transference of the plays from Corpus Christi to Whitsun. The clear reference to a three-day performance period is unique in the records of English Mystery Cycles and may be explained by the desire to exploit the holiday atmosphere for as long as possible and to solve the problems of overrunning the available playing time in one day caused by repeated performances of each play at each station. The surviving texts of the Chester plays are particularly long and even with the four or possibly five stations on the processional route would have required many hours to perform. Dividing the 25 plays into three sections to be performed on Monday, Tuesday and Wednesday of Whitsun week allowed for a reduced playing time each day for both audience and actors, who could therefore take advantage of the other attractions available at the Whitsun Fair, and also allowed for a reduction in the number of pageant wagons required. Many guilds shared a wagon with other guilds who performed a play on the other two days. Shortly after the first reference to the Whitsun Play, the Vintners, Goldsmith and Dyers made an agreement to share the wagon previously owned by the Vintners and Dyers. The Vintners were responsible for the play of *Herod and the Magi* which was performed on Monday, the Goldsmiths for the play of the *Slaughter of the Innocents*, performed on Tuesday, and the Dyers for the play of *Antichrist* which was performed on Wednesday. Each guild could therefore use the wagon when it was not being required by the other partners and reduce expenses for the maintenance, decoration and storage of a wagon. This particular sharing arrangement may have come about especially because each of the plays concerned requires a Palace as the setting and the same decoration and structure of the wagon could be used.[2]

The route for the Chester Whitsun Plays was from the Abbey Gates in Northgate Street, where each play was first performed before the Abbot and religious dignitaries, to the Prentice at High Cross, the next station where the Mayor and civic dignitaries watched the plays, to Watergate Street where another station was located and then to Bridge Street for the final performance. These details are contained in copies of David Rogers' *Brevary* which is a collection of notes on interesting features in Chester city life made by his father Robert Rogers (died 1595). Although details vary in different copies of the *Brevary* which David Rogers made in the early seventeenth century as he put into order and no doubt added to his father's papers, this route remains constant and may be interpreted as a first-hand account either by Robert Rogers or by an eye witness who reported to him. Other details in the Rogers' description of the plays are sometimes contradictory or confusing but they provide the main source for practical details of the organisation of the plays although they have been contaminated with what appears to be a 'local fiction' attributing the birth of the plays to the early fourteenth century and their authorship to Randall Higden, the noted Chester historian and author of the *Polychronicon*.[3] The *Brevary* also lists the plays and the guilds responsible for them as well as showing the division of the plays over three days. The first day saw the performance of the plays from the *Fall of Lucifer* (Barkers and Tanners) to the *Offering of the Magi* (Mercers and Spicers); the second day ran from the *Slaughter of the Innocents* (Goldsmiths and Masons) to the *Harrowing of Hell* (Cooks and Innkeepers); the third day began with the *Resurrection* (Skinners, Hatters, Girdlers) and ended with the *Last Judgement* (Weavers and Walkers).

According to Rogers, the plays were not necessarily played every year and when there was no performance a Midsummer Show was held instead. The Midsummer Show seems to have been a spectacular celebration using live exotic animals, models of giants and elements and characters from folk lore and folk celebration. At this show the trade guilds displayed characters and costumes from their plays, often with a child riding in a procession to represent them. In the years that the plays were given, on St George's Day the Banns were read to inform the population and to whet their interest for the performances later in the year. The town crier read the Banns, probably accompanied by a costumed rider in the manner of the Midsummer Show. The riders from each guild went in procession through the town and distributed money to prisoners at Northgate prison and in the Castle. The last performance of the Chester plays in 1575 was held during the Midsummer Show on one day in one location, probably at High Cross, possibly as a way of lightening the religious connotations of the cycle which had been arousing the displeasure and condemnation of the Church authorities.

Like all the complete cycles, the Chester plays end with a play on the Last Judgement or Doomsday. It is the final act in the representation of Christian history and provides a spectacular finale to the cycle which gathers the force of what the other plays have been showing and teaching in their portrayal of the Creation, the Fall, foreshadowings and life of Christ and the Passion as it affects the lives of the audience. The Corpus Christi Cycle celebrated the concept of salvation epitomised in the Corpus Christi Feast and Communion and its ultimate intention was to demonstrate that salvation in action. Throughout the cycle the audience had been invited to witness the mechanism of Christ's salvation of mankind through His sacrifice on the Cross and to understand the need for this Redemption. In the Doomsday Play, the audience is shown what happens to those who accept or reject the terms of this salvation, to those who recognise Christ and live according to His law and to those who choose rather to follow their own passions and senses in sin. The preceding plays of the cycle demonstrate why and how the choice is offered to mankind and the Doomsday Play shows the consequences of the choice.

In Christian terms, Doomsday or the Last Judgement is the final motivation for the individual soul's choice of good or evil. Those who prefer the things of this world will be damned forever with Satan and the Fallen Angels, those who choose the things of the spirit, which are the only currency in the next world, will be granted eternal bliss. The Christian religion offers Christ as a God of Mercy, a God who is ready to forgive mankind for its sin and arrogance. The concept of repentance for sin offers a hope of salvation even though earlier preferences, or mistakes, for material goods or pleasures may have been expressed. The threat inherent in Doomsday reconciles this tendency to allow for second thoughts and to live badly yet assure eternal bliss through a last-minute change of heart, holding repentance as a kind of insurance policy to be signed, if necessary, at the last moment. Repentance and recognition of Christ's sacrifice can lead to eternal bliss, but it must be sincere repentance based on practical evidence of good intentions in a holy life and good works.

The Bible sets out the form of the Last Judgement in Matthew 24, 25 and provides more lurid details in the Apocalypse or Book of Revelation. Here the emphasis is on the fact that no one can know when the Judgement will occur and all should therefore live in preparation to be called for reckoning. Matthew states the terms of the Judgement in a gathering and separation of mankind before the throne of Christ, the righteous will be placed on His right and be led to eternal life and the cursed, the evil souls, will be placed on the left to be taken to the everlasting fire prepared for the devil (Matthew, 24, 30–1; 25, 31–46). Although the Matthew account uses the imagery of animal husbandry in the image of the sheep – the righteous – being separated from the goats – the wicked – later theologians, and especially those of the Middle Ages, preferred to express the event in the imagery of a judicial trial, with Christ as Judge of conduct rather than herdsman, giving more importance to the moral questions involved in the life and choices of each soul to be judged, rather than bodily or physical characteristics.

In sermon and tract and in the visual arts, medieval religious thought gave much importance to the Last Judgement as a means of persuading and encouraging individuals to repent, to lead a holy life free from sin resisting the temptations of the world and to ensure themselves a place among the blessed. Because the Last Judgement was necessarily in the future many attempts were made to vitalise representations of it in order to bring its import home to those in the present. It was one of the most frequent subjects for wall paintings in medieval churches so that those who went to Mass could have their Faith and good intentions reinforced by grisly reminders of what awaited them and what followed from their present choices and actions. In visual representations of Doomsday once again the 'bad' side is given most attention and there are grotesque details of horrible demons and the torturers they will inflict on the wicked. In contrast, the good usually stand meek, still and repetitious with St Michael or Christ, showing none of the variety of types and interest of movement displayed by their wicked counterparts. Encouragement is offered by negative contrast; displaying the full details of what awaits the wicked demonstrates how peaceful and blissful will be the destiny of the blessed.

The Chester Doomsday Play works within the imagery of a civil trial, with Christ as Judge and mankind, the accused, represented by types of human classes and activities. Two Popes, Emperors, Kings and Queens and a Merchant and a Lawyer come before Christ to recount their lives and be judged accordingly. The Good Souls, though they confess to have sinned during their lives, plead to be considered eligible for eternal bliss on the grounds of their good works during their lives and the years they have spent in Purgatory to purge their sins. Christ accepts their plea and summons His angels to lead them to bliss. The Bad Souls have no extenuating circumstances for their sins were not offset by any good works during their lifetimes and two demons appear to make the case against them, using the language of sophistry and legal procedures to prove that God's righteousness must damn these souls according to what He had promised. The demons' language is full of pompous Latin quotations and the mannerisms of the courts:

> And, lest thou forgett, good man,
> I shall mynne thee upon,
> for speake Latten well I can,
> and that thou shall soone see.
>
> (ll. 561–4)[4]

The mock disputation was in all likelihood played in the manner of the courts, perhaps with the demons putting on lawyers' robes, stepping forth to present their case, indicating the wretched accused and using high rhetorical tone and gesture towards Christ. The theme would have been even more poignant as one of the 'accused' is a Lawyer who had taken on false causes for monetary gain in his lifetime.

Whereas many of the representations of the Last Judgement in the pictorial arts use the iconography of the weighing of the souls by St Michael before Christ, drawing out the image of the Scales of Justice, all the plays choose the courtroom imagery. A legal dispute is obviously much more dramatic; it can capture the attention of the audience as points are argued and defended, creating suspense as to the outcome of the final judgement and sentence. Dialogue replaces iconography. It must also be remembered that a physical weighing of souls would have been difficult to stage, requiring at least a prop scales machinery large enough to accommodate several souls. The Last Judgement Plays do involve spectacular effects with at least two playing levels, trumpets and usually a lift mechanism for the descent of Christ, but the scales would be bulky, unwieldy and essentially static. Scales too would allow sins and virtues of the souls being judged to be expressed only in the abstract terms of relative weight, with no physical details as is possible in the court-room setting with the details of previous lives being given as evidence. In the Last Judgement Plays, dialogue has been chosen over iconography not merely as the more inherently dramatic technique but also in order to point the lesson of the play. The audience must be able to identify with the souls being judged and relate what happens to them in the play, damnation or salvation, to what will happen to *them* at the Day of Doom. The details of the souls' lives provide a means of recognition, they have done, or not done, things which the members of the audience may themselves have done or have been tempted not to do. Like the recognisable everyday Shepherds to whom the promise of salvation was first made known and the workmen of the Crucifixion more concerned with solving problems caused by poor materials than with recognising the moral responsibility of their actions, the damned and saved souls reflect elements of the life or knowledge of the members of the audience so that they might apprehend the spiritual meaning the plays represent and apply it to their own lives.

The audience has a central role in the Last Judgement Play, for the direction of the play is focused entirely on the individual Christian souls which the members of the audience represent. The other plays in the cycle recount events and characters of the biblical narrative, or apocryphal additions to it such as the Nativity Midwives or the Assumption of the Virgin, but the Last Judgement Play shows things which have not yet happened and which are indicated only as future events in the Bible itself. Apart from Christ and in some cases St Michael, there are no specific biblical characters in this play whose stories are known, whose part in the Christian scheme of history is familiar. In this play, the audience is shown itself in a hypothetical yet inevitable future situation for which it must be persuaded to prepare. In this play past, present and future converge to create a powerful emphasis and persuasion by example on the life and mind of the audience. The earthly characters of this play are types of the audience, not historical or biblical characters. When Christ, in the Chester play, makes his address to 'the good and evil souls here present', He is addressing the audience as much as the characters grouped on or around the pageant wagon:

You good and evell that here benne lent,
here you come to your judgment,
yf you wyst whereto hit would appent
and in what manere.
But all myne, as I have ment –
prophettes, patriarches here present –
must knowe my doome with good intent.
Therefore I am nowe here.

(ll. 357–64)

The repetition of the direct address and the personal pronoun 'you' throughout this central speech emphasises that this lesson is intended for the audience, and the switch to the singular 'thou' and 'thee' in the stanzas relating the cause of Christ's birth and sacrifice to mankind's sin makes the point even more immediate and personal (ll. 369–84).

As Christ recounts the motivation for His Passion and the suffering He underwent to redeem mankind there is a conscious parallel made to the address from the Cross in the Crucifixion Plays where Christ drew mankind's attention to His suffering. Now, Christ standing in Judgement has come to determine if mankind has accepted that gift or not, to see if that suffering has been in vain. The Chester play heightens this climactic moment with a spectacular piece of stage business in which Christ's wounds bleed as He tells the details of the Passion. As in the York Crucifixion Play, this was no doubt achieved through the careful placing of sachets or bladders of paint which were squeezed to emit the 'blood'. Christ's speech gives the build up to the flow of blood until after the direct command to 'all men' to look and see the blood flow 'for your salvatyon' (ll. 425–8); the Latin stage direction indicates that the blood flows and the final stanza of the speech projects a further series of impassioned 'you' addresses. It is a moment of high dramatic tension and is concluded as Christ urges 'eych man' to think on what he has seen and to recognise that the righteous who accept the terms of Christ's sacrifice will come to bliss in the Judgement which now follows.

The representatives of mankind in the Chester Judgement Play may not be felt to be truly representative for they are taken from the upper levels of the social hierarchy rather than from the more humble ranks of everyday life. They can perhaps be seen as more generically representative if they are understood as types of this world's attempts at organisation and power. The Kings, Emperors and Popes are figures from the apogee of the social, political and religious power structures of this world, the extreme points of influence, status and domination to which any can aspire and by the whims of whom any can be affected in their daily life. The demonstration that these super powers are also subject to judgement and, more importantly, condemnation, before God in the Doomsday Play effectively implies that in spiritual terms such hierarchies have no value and that the only value scales which should be considered by the individual Christian soul are those espoused by the Christian religion, that is, love of God expressed through loving treatment of fellow men, the good works which Christ expounds at the moment of Judgement. All those who do not treat their fellow men as they would treat their God but according to worldly scales of value, be they of position, wealth or status, will be condemned. The two 'bad' figures in the Chester play, the Merchant and the Lawyer, have no good equivalents which suggests that they were a later addition to the play in an attempt to concretise the concepts of worldly power and status in figures more immediately relevant to the audience. The urge of the play is to persuade by bad example and so it may have been felt that these two figures did not necessarily require good counterparts in order to achieve their effect, but there may also be a certain amount of social satire in the denigration of these two influential types of power and corruption in town life with no redeeming features.

The Towneley-Wakefield Last Judgement Play is directed towards concrete social satire rather than abstract hierarchies. Although the social types to be condemned or saved are not given direct speaking parts in which to state their case as they are in Chester, the Devils who are to lead away the lost souls give many details of the trades whose members are ripe for condemnation as they anticipate their share of the Judgement decision. As the Devils make their way to the Judgement carrying the 'rentals', the books in which all the sins of mankind have been recorded, and the bags in which sins have been stored, they meet Tutivillus, a wandering devil who makes his report on his research on sinners in the world, listing the types of sin he found and where he found them. Ale-houses have yielded especially rich pickings and the

Lollards have provided him with a lot of material as have followers
of fashion who give more importance to their appearance than to
their souls. The Towneley-Wakefield audience is in this way led
to recognise the sins of the lost souls as those they themselves may
be guilty of, particularly as they watch the play on a holiday
occasion when they may well be tempted to pass some time in the
ale-house and are probably dressed in their best clothes. They
then have their identity with the sinners made explicit as Tutivillus
turns to them and his description becomes direct address:

> And ye lanettys of the stewys and lychoures on lofte
> youre baill now brewys . . .
> . . . welcom to my see![5]

What the Towneley-Wakefield play lacks, however, is any persuasion through positive example and while the satire and humour
of the Devils' conversation is dramatically effective, its very human
attractiveness works against a strong pointing of the moral of the
Doomsday Play, for the chatty, joking Devils have little power to
terrify.

The audience then has a special role in the Judgement Plays for
it is by implication a collective member of the cast. The events of
the play take place not in an historical past but in a hypothetical
future which is a direct consequence of the present of the audience.
Members of the audience must choose how to live their lives,
aided by the events they have seen played out in the cycle and
reinforced by the final demonstration of the consequences of this
choice at the Day of Judgement. Their choices will decide on
which part of the scene they will be standing at the Day of
Judgement, on the right of God being led to glory and eternal
bliss or on the left being dragged away in chains by the Devils
down to Hell Mouth and eternal agony. Their presence in this
scenario, in an as yet unspecified future moment, is assured, it is
up to them to decide their positioning. As an aid to decision all
the Judgement plays offer an emphasis on Christ's Passion and
the contemplation of its significance for the audience's future. As
Christ descends to make His Judgement in the Chester play, He
recounts the details of the Crucifixion and the Angels hold up and
show to both the souls and the audience the instruments of the
Passion. In all likelihood these would have been painted boards

or banners showing the Cross, the crown of thorns, the spear, the sponge, the hammer and the nails.[6] In this reference back to the central action of the cycle there is also a reference to the reasons for the Passion in the Fall of Man and to the prophets and patriarchs who lived before Christ's coming, thereby inviting the audience to recall the early plays of the cycle and drawing together the whole sequence. The play opens with an even stronger parallel to the beginning of the cycle which emphasises the universality of the play's relevance as Christ repeats the opening line of the Creation Play:

Ego sum alpha et omega, I, primus et novissimus
(l. 1 and Play I, l. 1)

In the beginning is the end and so the members of the audience must recognise that God's time is universal and that as Man's Fall was redeemed by Christ's sacrifice, so their sins in life can be redeemed by accepting the offer of salvation, repenting and living a life of good works.

As the final play in the cycle sequence and the climactic exhortatory moment of the moral message of the cycle, the Judgement Play invited spectacle effects, elaboration and decoration to bring the cycle and the teaching to an arresting ending. The biblical account of the Judgement provides an inspiration for spectacular staging effects for Matthew states that the end of the world will be predicted by war, famine, earthquakes, martyrdoms, betrayals and false prophets, followed by a darkening of heaven and earth and the descent of Christ 'in the clouds of heaven with power and great glory' as mankind is summoned by angels sounding a trumpet (24, 30–1). The medieval playwrights certainly did not ignore the invitation to spectacle and special staging effects which Matthew's account offers. It is significant that this play was the responsibility of the richest and most powerful guild in the cities for which details survive. During the late fifteenth and early sixteenth centuries the richest guilds were usually those connected with the cloth trade, the main source of England's wealth in this period. In York, the Judgement Play was performed by the Mercers, traders in cloth and other associated products, in Coventry by the Drapers and in Chester by the Websters or weavers. These were guilds which would have had the financial resources to support high costs of costuming and decoration for wagons as well as to provide the stage machinery and special effects which the events of the play suggest.

An important document surviving from York which indicates the many details of the staging of the Judgement Plays is the Mercers' Indenture.[7] This is a record of the props belonging to the Mercers' Pageant in 1433, for which the Pageant Masters were responsible and which they had to return to the guild after their term of office. The document comes from a relatively early stage of the Mystery Cycles and already indicates elaborate details of performance. The play requires three locations, Heaven, Hell and the place of Judgement which is usually considered to be Earth for 'secundum doctoris opiniones, in aere prope terram judicabit Filius Dei' (following l. 355). Heaven would be on an upper level of the wagon from whence God as Christ would speak at the beginning of the play, as He had at the beginning of the Creation Play, thereby matching the verbal parallel of the opening lines of both plays with a visual parallel. The Souls would be on the Earth level which in all probability was represented by the floor of the wagon and the Devils and the Bad Souls issuing from Hell would have been at the ground level. Hell would have been represented by a Hell Mouth which was probably a separate structure placed to the side of the main wagon. The Mercers' Indenture lists 'A heuen of Iren with a naffe of tree' (a Heaven made of iron with a wooden roof (?)) and 'iiij irens to bere vppe heuen' (4 pieces of iron to hold Heaven up). The first item on the list is a 'Pageant with iiij wheles', the pageant wagon itself, and this is followed by reference to a 'helle mouthe'. The Hell Mouth would therefore seem to be a structure rather than a painting, as it follows the pageant wagon and comes before the costumes and masks in the list. Christ descends to make the Judgement and then reascends to heaven and at York at least this method of descent was provided in the form of a swing or an iron frame lowered by ropes: 'A brandreth of Iren þat god sall sitte uppon when he sall sty vppe to heuen with iiij rapes at iiij corners'. The Matthew passage states that Christ shall come in clouds of glory to the Judgement and the York Mercers had eight clouds, some blue, some red and some with sunbeams and stars. Clouds feature in the Chester play too where there is the stage direction that Christ should descend in a cloud, 'quasi in nube', although the difficulty of this manoeuvre is acknowledged in the qualifier: 'if it can be done' (si fieri poterit). A lift mechanism like the York swing, decorated with clouds, could have been used or perhaps if the engineering skills of the Websters were not sufficient for such feats, a ladder could have been fixed between the upper and floor level of the wagon, hidden behind wooden prop clouds.

The trumpets which feature in Matthew's account of the Judgement were used in the plays. The Mercers' Indenture lists 'two trumpets of white plate [steel?]' while the Towneley-Wakefield play makes frequent references to the sounding of the trumpet as the Devils hurry to the place of Judgement, fearing lest they be late for the trumpet sounded a long time ago. In the Chester play, two Angels blow trumpets to awaken the souls of the dead: ·

> Tunc angeli tubas accipient et flabunt, et
> omnes mortui de sepulchris surgent . . .
> (following l. 40)

A sharp contrast in costuming was made between the good characters and the bad. Angels and God would be dressed in white with gilded masks while the Devils would have been dressed in colourful, extravagant costumes probably with animal features and possibly with fireworks attached to them.[8] The Chester souls would have been dressed to reflect their earthly status at least as far as their headgear was concerned, with crowns for the monarchs and the three-tiered crown for the two Popes. Visual representations of the Judgement usually represent the souls as naked, yet with crowns or hair. The Chester souls arise from their tombs, possibly small tomb-like structures placed on the wagon or even a trap door in the floor of the wagon. The close-fitting vests and tights referred to in the Mercers' Indenture recall the costumes listed for Adam and Eve in the Norwich records which were supposed to represent them in their pre-Fall nakedness. Some kind of colour contrast would have been used to distinguish the good from the bad.[9] The four Evangelists who appear at the end of the Chester play to point the moral of the play and stress that they had given good warning in their works would have been dressed in white with gilded masks and, as the Mercers' Indenture indicates, crowns and yellow wigs. It is tempting to think that possibly some ghoulish details of costuming were made at least for the Chester Bad

Queen, who makes so many references to her former love of fine clothes, furs, jewels and cosmetics which led her to the sin of Pride and to provocation to Lechery in others:

> Of lecherye I never wrought,
> but ever to that synne I sought,
> that of that fylth in deede and thought
> yett had I never that fyll.
>
> Fye on pearles! Fye on prydee!
> Fye on gowne! Fye on guyde!
> Fye on hewe! Fye on hyde!
> These harrowe me to hell.
>
> (ll. 273–80)

Perhaps this character was costumed as a cadaver or with a particularly hideous mask in order to point the contrast between the earthly life and the other-worldly destiny. The York Mercers' God had a close-fitting garment showing the stigmata of the Crucifixion and it is probable that the Chester God as Christ was similarly apparelled with sachets of paint concealed behind the wounds to bleed at the appropriate moment (ll. 425–8).

The Good Souls would be escorted to Heaven by the Angels, singing in the Chester play, possibly ascending to the upper level of the wagon by the ladder (a swing mechanism would accommodate only one character) or simply by being led away stage right implicitly to Heaven, behind the wagon side curtain. The Bad Souls would then be led off by the Devils, stage left to a Hell Mouth, if such a structure were used. The Chester dialogue includes several references to the fires of Hell and it is possible that smoke or fireworks were used to represent a Hell location. The twelfth-century Anglo-Norman play *Le Mistere d'Adam* gives the stage direction to 'make a great smoke to arise' in Hell as Adam and Eve are received into Hell and most pictorial representations of the Judgement and the Harrowing of Hell show smoke issuing from the Hell Mouth or Hell Dungeon.[10]

The Last Judgement Play concludes the cycle with a spectacular flourish and an exclusive focus on the audience as implicit characters. In using non-biblical characters to point the lesson of the audience's need to consider its end and its own judgement, this play comes very close to the techniques of the Morality plays.[11] Outside the known events of biblical history the audience sees itself placed on the stage and its own life put under examination. The human characters of the Last Judgement Play are divided into representative types of good and evil, the only characters presented as types in the Mystery plays. The Last Judgement Play shows the outcome of the battle for the individual Christian's soul as a sharp reminder to the members of the audience to apply the lessons they have seen in the preceding plays to their moral life. Details of the battle and the practical forms it can take in the audience's own world become the subject matter for the Morality plays.

PART II
Moralities and Interludes

6
Didactic Drama: 'Everyman' and other Morality Plays

The first records of Morality plays, of which the most widely known is *Everyman*, occur at around the same time as the Mystery Cycles were being performed by the trade guilds. It is at first easier to see the differences between the two types of play rather than their similarities. The Morality is not concerned with Bible history and is not cyclical in form. Nevertheless, both forms are unashamedly didactic drama and both are deeply concerned for the spiritual welfare of man. Because the Morality was not tied to the static theology of the scriptures which shaped the Mystery play, it is in many ways a more flexible dramatic form. The driving force behind any Morality play was to teach – but the personal views of the author (most usually an unknown writer) towards social, political, religious or moral matters were incorporated into a set of conventions which that writer in turn both inherited and expanded. For this reason there is no such thing as a 'typical' Morality play – a fact which is at the same time both exhilarating and exasperating.

Even the use of the term Morality play is marked by this tantalising ambivalence: as a genre devised by modern critics it seems to cover those plays which treat moral ideas didactically, through the use of personified dramatis personae. It is not a term which would have been found in use in the period whence the plays originate, when the term 'interlude' was used. The Interlude includes dramatic entertainments of many diverse forms and could have been applied to plays with or without a moral theme.

Morality plays have been called the 'drama of moral instruction',[1] and their instructional nature is felt to have a kinship with the sermon or homiletic literature of their period. They showed primarily how the individual human soul was tempted by the devil into sinfulness and how salvation could be gained through penitence. The preachers, artists and dramatic writers of the fifteenth century all relied on similar imagery to depict their message either in words, pictures or in the animate form of theatrical representation.

If the momentum behind the growth of Morality plays was a homiletic one, the extension of the work of Franciscan and Dominican friars must have been influential. Their use of the allegorical *exemplum* in preaching is a parallel to the allegorical methods of the plays. The term allegory needs some elaboration here, as it is often misunderstood by a modern readership. It is not unusual for allegory to be considered to work almost exclusively by personification: one reason for this is that the dramatis personae in the allegorical drama of Morality plays are personifications. But, while personification is a means of endowing qualities and ideas with an animate existence, they are not allegories in themselves. Personifications can be understood quite literally: when Everyman is called 'Everyman' that is precisely what he presents. Similarly with Fellowship, Kindred and so on. Allegory is metaphorical in its basis and consists of a complex web of metaphors arranged in narrative form.

The term 'abstract' has been avoided in this description of allegory quite deliberately. It is a misleading and somewhat unmedieval concept in this context. For, in the religious, hierarchical world of the medieval period a separation between the so-called real world and the world of abstract ideas would turn reality on its head. For Aristotle and subsequently for the Medieval period, the whole universe was a hierarchy whereby God at the top is pure form – pure actuality – and at the bottom is our world of matter, which is mere potentiality. Reality consists not in the material world around us, but in the eternal principles such as truth, goodness and beauty; real entities, not just abstract names.

A number of points which relate to our notions of drama should be made with regard to this use of allegory. The first is that the opposition which we make between 'real' characters and personifications needs to be set aside in terms of Morality plays and, moreover, in terms of the later Elizabethan drama too. Since the world was perceived as a great analogy which made apparent the otherwise unseen reality of God, a contemporary audience would readily accept personified figures appearing with historical, biblical personages or contemporary figures. The most relevant example of this phenomenon in the context of *Everyman* is the N-Town Death of Herod Play where, in addition to being a particular historical person, Herod, the character acquires a more universal quality, as King of Life. This comes about through his interaction with the personified Death, when Death comes to claim him, since this interaction draws on an allegorical tradition. Similarly mid-sixteenth-century plays have personifications and historical characters in the same action. Death, the Mower, appears at the end of Marlowe's *Edward the Second*. In Shakespeare's *Titus Andronicus* the division between 'real' and 'personified' is fluid, as the character Tamara appears in the familiar likeness of Revenge at the close of the play.

A further issue which should be considered is that of the acting style appropriate to personification drama. Allied to the critical opposition just discussed, and dismissed, between real and allegorical characters there has grown up a further critical opposition relating to acting styles. Critics have suggested that unlike the realistic style of modern acting, medieval and Renaissance theatre relied on an acting style which was 'formal' in method.[2] The *Chirologia* and *Chironomia* of John Bulwer (1644) have been pressed into service to support this view. These manuals, it is claimed, provide evidence of a formal system of gestures being employed on stage. In fact it is probable that many of the gestures Bulwer illustrates would not be recognised as formal even by a modern audience. Hands held together with fingers pressed against each other is a quite natural gesture of prayer or pleading. It would be misleading to suggest an acting style which would be exaggerated, akin to modern mime: the medieval stage was not peopled by wooden actors. It is far more likely that there was sufficient width in the acting styles employed to allow the actor to build the outer form, the dramatis persona, as a discrete living being and to bring forward when appropriate the universality of the role.

The longest of the fifteenth-century Morality plays, *The Castle of Perseverance*, uses a variety of allegories, and it is shaped by the way in which these allegories are employed to work together. The allegorical castle is, of course, a form which is central to this play, and it was no less a commonplace of the medieval pulpit. The most widely known of the literary castle allegories was Bishop Grossteste's *Le Chasteau d'Amour*, where the allegory involves many of the forces which also appear in *The Castle of Perseverance*. Both are bounded by a ditch or moat and both castles are involved in protecting the human protagonist, the soul, from the Seven Deadly Sins, who are ruled by the World, the Flesh and the Devil. the second most important allegorical feature is the battle of the vices and virtues. This is adapted to the form of a siege in *The Castle of Perseverance*, an appropriate use of the form when allied to the castle imagery. This battle allegory gives the play something of a kinship with the *Psychomachia* of Prudentius, but it would be inappropriate to stretch the similarities very far, as there are many ways in which the *Psychomachia* is inappropriate. In the Latin poem the vices and virtues are represented as female, since these abstract names take feminine gender. It would be silly to have all the vices and virtues as female in dramatic form. It is doubtful whether women took part in dramatic entertainments at all in the medieval period. Nevertheless, for the climactic point of fending off the assault the play borrows the Latin poem's image of throwing roses for this crucial piece of action.

Further allegorical commonplaces used by *The Castle of Perseverance* are the Debate of the Four Daughters of God and the allegorical journey. The best known journey is Deguilleville's *Le Pèlerinage de la vie Humaine*, translated into English by Lydgate, among others. In the *Castle* it is certainly clear that Humanum Genus is on a journey toward eternity through a moral landscape. This large-scale Morality play can thus be seen as a blending of a variety of allegorical features. The method used is akin to that of montage, which obliges spectators themselves to create meaning from what is presented. The allegories, common enough through sermon and pictorial analogues, thus become a means of dramatising the issues of salvation and of demonstrating the progress of the human soul. While the Moralities are not necessarily episodic in the sense that the Mystery plays so clearly are, nonetheless, they do demonstrate a blending of elements, offering a shape which appears at times incomplete and incoherent, but which relies primarily on its audience to interact with its loose mod construction to create its meaning and experience its truth. The journey and another form – that of the summoning account – are employed together to shape the play which has fixed itself in the modern mind as the Morality play *par excellence, Everyman*. In this fusion the Ars Moriendi, the art of dying, has been extremely influential, as has the Danse Macabre, an allegory conceived as a dance of the living and the dead. *Everyman* is a play which is drawn from a European culture obsessed with death, a Europe which had been gripped by the plague and in which death was the great leveller who comes to every man. Everyman is summoned in his turn to undertake a long and difficult journey, to render his account. Strength, riches, friendship and beauty will be of no help – death comes to all, regardless.

That *Everyman*[3] has been the most popular and best known of Morality plays in modern times is indisputable. Why this should be so is an interesting object of enquiry in its own right. It must be stated here that there are some essential differences between *Everyman* and many of the other Morality plays, and while it may shape the modern conception of what a Morality play is, *Everyman* should in no sense be regarded as typical. For, whereas many Morality plays retell the struggles of an erring Mankind who falls into wickedness and is then, at length, restored to virtue, *Everyman* is wholly concerned with one moment – that of the Coming of Death – a moment infused with intense emotional impact. This is a moment which forms part of the action in some of the other plays, most notably in *The Castle of Perseverance* and in *The Pride of Life* and it is useful to compare the treatments offered there.

The Pride of Life is fragmentary and it is in the lost conclusion of the play that Death appears and slays the King of Life. The Prologue, however, tells the story and gives a flavour of the action:

> Deth comith, he dremith a dredfful dreme–
> Welle aȝte al carye;
> And slow ffader and moder and þen heme:
> He ne wold none sparye.

> Sone affter hit befel þat Deth and Life
> Beth togeder itaken;

And ginnith and striuith a sterne strife,
[þe] King of Life to wrake.[4]

The most terrifying moment in *The Castle of Perseverance* is the Coming of Death, who strikes Humanum Genus to the heart with his dart, the familiar iconographic characteristic of his role. His speech takes on some of the qualities associated with a Complaint of the Times, looking back to a better age, contrasted to the impoverished time now:

> In the grete pestelens
> Thanne was I wel knowe.
> But now al-most I am forgete;
> Men of Deth holde no tale.
> (ll. 2838–42)

In both plays the Mankind figure dies in a state of sin. The intercession of the Virgin Mary is prompted by the soul's contrition in *The Pride of Life*. In *The Castle of Perseverance*, by crying out for Mercy at the hour of his death, Mankind enables Mercy to plead on his behalf in the set piece debate of the four Daughters of God (though it is clear from the Banns that an alternative ending involving Mary's intercession may have been envisaged at one time). Both plays thus show the power of contrition even on the point of death.

The atypical qualities of *Everyman* may be a result of its relationship to the Dutch play *Elckerlijc*. It is usually assumed that the Dutch play was the original, and that *Everyman* is an English reworking. Whatever the order of priority, it is clear that the connection between the two places the English play firmly within the framework of continental religious thought. In particular, the ideas of the Northern European Reform movement, known as the Devotio Moderna, are given clear expression within the play. In reaction against the formalism and laxity of so many of their contemporaries, whom they perceived as going through the motions of religious ceremony and paying lip-service to belief, groups of fervent believers sought to move away from the abuses and the malpractices and found a movement based on common-sense mysticism, the ideal of a simple life of prayer, ascetic self-denial and charitable works.

This new direction in spirituality is given moving expression in *The Imitation of Christ*, usually attributed to Thomas à Kempis.[5] Here is an extract which is pertinent to the concerns of *Everyman*:

> Blessed is the man who keeps the hour of his death always before him in his mind, and daily prepares himself to die. . . . Be ready at all times, and so live that death may never find you unprepared. . . . Do not rely on friends and neighbours and do not delay the salvation of your soul to some future date, for men will forget you sooner than you think.

In *Everyman*, Death tells us:

> Lo, yonder I see Everyman walking
> Full little he thinketh on my coming;
> (ll. 81–2)

and when he summons Everyman to make his reckoning the man replies:

> O Death, thou comest when I had thee least in mind!
> (l. 119)

The urgent lesson for fifteenth-century Europeans, living in the constant shadow of death by plague is given in meditative form in the *Imitation* and in dramatic form in *Everyman*:

> High the office and great the dignity of a priest to whom is granted what is not granted to Angels; for only a rightly ordained priest has the power to celebrate the Eucharist and to hallow the body of Christ.

This emphasis on the importance of the priestly function of consecrating the Eucharist makes it clear that the author of the *Imitation* was very far from being an early Protestant. His views are squarely within the Catholic tradition. *Everyman* follows this line in its assertion that the clergy are above angels in degree, since they administer the holy sacrament.

FIVE WITS: For priesthood exceedeth all other thing:
. . .
God hath to them more power given
Than to any angel that is in heaven.
With five words he may consecrate,
God's body in flesh and blood to make,
And handleth his Maker between his hands.
(ll. 732,735–9)

The play is a dramatisation of the timeless and universal problem of dying in a state of grace but this strong assertion of the importance of the Church's institutional role in saving human souls shows its contemporary social allegiances with the orthodox reform movement of the period.

In addition to the assertion that the priesthood is above angels in degree, we have the castigation of those clergy who abuse their office:

KNOWLEDGE: Sinful priests giveth the sinners
example bad;
Their children sitteth by other men's fires,
(ll. 759–60)

This concern with priests who bring their office into disrepute is common to much medieval literature – *Piers Plowman*,[6] for example shows Sloth as a priest (C Text, Passus 7, ll. 30–2). It would be very wrong to interpret such remarks as damning the clergy generally – for it is clear that in *Everyman* such clergy are regarded as the aberrant exception, rather than the rule. The institutional role of the Church in man's salvation structures *Everyman*, and the play clearly places its weight behind the importance of the intervention of the clergy in the redemption of humanity. Thus the seven sacraments are carefully explained to the audience in lines 722–7.

The message was urgent in the fifteenth century, for the abuses and misconduct of some members of the clergy had led to increasing disaffection among worshippers. Further, the four stages of penance prescribed by the Church are dwelt upon: Confession, Contrition, Absolution and Satisfaction. Salvation is thus linked to the role of the clergy and the message is thus primarily a theological and highly ideological one.

Everyman is not just a call to obedience; it has not been written merely to extol the system. Linked to its roots in the Devotio Moderna, the play offers clear evidence of the religious vitality of a lay piety, with an interest in prayer, devotion and practical religion. The Devotio Moderna is concerned with personal reflection and spiritual introspection and places the onus on the individual to foster a direct and personal faith. Contemplation on Christ's Passion found new fervour at this time. We are instructed in the *Imitation*:

> Remember your avowed purpose, and keep ever before you the likeness of Christ crucified.

Perhaps the most famous meditation on the Passion for an English reader is that of Julian of Norwich in *The Revelation of Divine Love*:[7]

> For I could see that the great, hard, hurtful nails in those dear and tender hands and feet caused the wounds to gape wide and the body to sag forward under its own weight, and because of the time it hung there. His head was scarred and torn and the crown was sticking to it, congealed with blood.

The message to contemplate Christ's Passion is succinctly combined with the Ars Moriendi theme in a medieval lyric[8] which adapts a line from the response of the eighth lesson in the offices of the dead: Terribilis mors Conturbat Me (Fearful death confounds me).

In *Everyman* the drama guides its audience in the art of dying by placing the sequence of human life and death in consonance with the redeeming life and death of Christ, and thereby with salvation. Robert Potter[9] explains the process, pointing out that, 'Everyman, denied (like Christ) by all, yet sustained by good deeds, and bound (with Christ) in the sacraments, dies in a state of Grace. His last thoughts are of Christ's redeeming death and his last words (from the sacrament of extreme unction) are Christ's last words: In manus tuas commendo spiritum meum' (cf. ll. 886–7). The play itself ends in a manner reminiscent of some of the Judgement plays, repeating Christ's words to unrepentant sinners:

Ite maledicti, in ignem eternum.

(l. 915)

For this play, which encapsulates the lonely moment of Death, is, like the Judgement plays of the Mystery Cycles, a drama of last things – of Death, Judgement, Heaven and Hell.

Most commentators agree that *Everyman* is not a typical English Morality play and yet it is the one example of the form which has left an indelible impression on modern times. Some have claimed that this is due to its superior quality, that it is a Morality *par excellence*, which displays how great the form can be, and often those same commentators denigrate the form as a whole as lewd, clumsy and inartistic. Such commentators seem to be concerned above all with establishing *Everyman* as an absolute by which the other plays are measured, in much the way that in Renaissance drama, Shakespeare is the absolute by which other playwrights are judged. A different perspective is needed, one which highlights how the play addressed its audience and how it placed its viewers. While not assuming an ideal viewer, or claiming that what is postulated here for the play was necessarily intended by the authors, it is nevertheless true that the contemporary spectators of the play created meanings relevant to the conditions in which they lived. These can be generated from the text in the ways outlined above. *Everyman* in the twentieth century has been read in a somewhat different way for a variety of reasons. The twentieth-century spectator or critic brings his or her own cultural assumptions to the play, and these too should be examined in relation to the meanings that they invoke in the play, since if we do not use them, they tend to use us.

Robert Potter has highlighted the fact that the first modern revival of a Morality play was of *Everyman* and that this production was highly influential on a number of people actively engaged in the drama of the twentieth century, among them George Bernard Shaw, William Butler Yeats and Max Reinhardt.[10] The man responsible for the production was William Poel, a radical anti-quarian, and the first staging was in 1901. It was recreated by Reinhardt in a German version, *Jedermann*, in a political guise and further had a formative influence on some of the religious drama of the twentieth century, most notably T. S. Eliot's *Murder in the Cathedral*. Eric Bentley, writing on the epic theatre of the twentieth century and its chief exponent, Bertolt Brecht, has found that this too has its origins in the modern notion of a Morality play:

> Obsessed with religion – a subject he could not keep away from for more than a few pages at a time – he often thought in terms of traditional religious abstraction. He wrote a Seven Deadly Sins and talked of writing a Dance of Death. His 'invention', the Lehrstuck, is a sort of catholic Morality play revised by a Marxist reader of Luther's Bible.[11]

Everyman has indeed travelled on a long journey. The play staged by Poel varied in important ways from the text of *Everyman* we have discussed in this chapter. An examination of the prompt copies used by Poel, which are held in the Enthoven Collection of the Victoria and Albert Museum, demonstrate that many of the passages which directly indicate the ideological concerns of the play have been cut from the version which found its way into production. While this may have made the play more approachable to a modern audience we must recognise that the meaning made available to them was significantly different to that in the original play text. The text would therefore only permit certain kinds of response, and these would be significantly at odds with those available to an audience contemporary with the play, both because of the different social contexts and concerns of the fifteenth and twentieth centuries and further because of the changes imposed on the text by Poel. It is as well to be aware of these things and to understand the differences.

The success of *Everyman* has produced a problematical result, as it has meant that, for the twentieth century, a flourishing tradition spanning several centuries has been boiled down into one play from which crucial passages have been cut and which is more a kind of Pre-Raphaelite construction, rather than anything truly representative of the genre. Nevertheless a debt is owed to Poel for having the inspiration to attempt a staging.

7
The Place

Plays differ from the purely literary arts as they take place in spatial locations and can use visual imagery and physical movement. The written play text needs a stage context and it shows its dependence on the physical conditions of performance, particularly on the actor's ability to portray discourse within the dramatic space.

The dramatic presentations of Morality plays appear to have been diverse and show the form's allegiances both to the acting traditions of cyclical and panoramic or arena methods of production and also to the non-dramatic itinerant preaching tradition. They rely on the distinction between localised and unlocalised playing areas – 'locus' and 'platea' – though the delineations of these two areas are diverse and vary according to the scale and nature of the play. Some of the smaller scale performances may be inn-yard plays, possibly relying on the use of a booth stage for the localised space. Plays of varying scope were produced in the indoor hall setting, and we also have clear evidence of large-scale place-and-scaffold playing in *The Castle of Perseverance*. The itinerant nature of many of the plays is clear, and the need to adapt readily to different staging conditions must have been one of the most basic demands to be met by the troupes of players responsible for production.

Everyman, one of the smaller scale Morality plays, demonstrates very well the flexibility of dramatic spectacle which is a hallmark of the Morality play. The staging requirements are so open that it could as well be staged outdoors on an open platea, on a booth-

and-trestle stage or in a hall. The requirements for performance are very simple, calling for no special effects or elaborate costuming. The original text has few stage directions but the staging appears to require a high place from which God and an angel speak, an unlocalised area and a scaffold, or localised area, representing the house of salvation or Church. Everyman has to descend into a grave: a trap-door would therefore be useful.

The Poel production of *Everyman* staged in 1901 had a remarkable impact, not least because of this direct and simple appeal. Newspaper accounts show how the performance broke with every existing theatre tradition held dear by early twentieth-century theatre-goers. It was a daytime outdoor performance in the courtyard of the Charterhouse, with spectators placed at windows, as well as on the ground area. The characters entered and exited through the ranks of the audience and on a level with them, and there was no distinctive lighting to distinguish performers and audience. In other words, the illusionistic practices on which Victorian theatre depended were completely missing. The set was a multi-levelled structure set against the outside of the great hall. The upper, battlemented level represented heaven and the lower level showed a domestic interior. On a separate locus 40 feet away a small chapel was placed, and the action moved between these two fixed loci. Poel's feel for place-and-scaffold playing provided a set appropriate to the dramatic tenets of the play.

While the reconstruction stopped short of presenting the play fully, in the ways mentioned in the previous chapter (largely it appears because of a twentieth-century fastidiousness concerning what religious ceremonies can be represented in drama), the production demonstrated the staging potential of a play which had been considered dull and lifeless. The critic for the *Athaneum* wrote:

> The primitive drama, which seems so full and didactic, may well have passioned our forefathers . . . is, indeed, capable of passioning us.[1]

Indoor staging, generally called Hall drama, is most particularly associated with Interludes, including Moral Interludes of the Tudor period, though there are some strong indications that entertainments occurred in halls at earlier periods also. What these entertainments were is more difficult to establish. Visiting minstrels, *histriones* or *lusores* are recorded from early times, but precisely what they did is not clear, as the terms 'play' and 'game' covered a multitude of different activities, including recitation, playing musical instruments and mumming as well as play-acting. In the Tudor period we can associate plays with places and dates of performance. We know, for example, that *Fulgens and Lucres* was written by Henry Medwall, whose patron was Archbishop Morton and that the play is likely to have been performed at Lambeth Palace, probably for the occasion of Prince Arthur's betrothal to Catherine of Aragon in 1497. The staging conditions of Hall drama relate specifically to the nature of indoor production.

Outdoor performance of Morality plays must have been diverse with regard to the spectacle they offered, but all seem to share certain basic staging principles. Medieval staging conventions can be traced as far back as the tenth-century liturgical drama, which developed from the divine services of the Church. These along with all other forms of medieval drama share a convention which distinguishes in terms of staging between localised and unlocalised playing areas. The localised area could be variously named as a 'locus' or 'sedes' in Latin and as a 'mansion' or 'scaffold' in English. The unlocalised area was called 'platea' in Latin and 'place' in English. The distinction between the two meant that the action which took place at a scaffold – a raised area – would be associated with a specific locality, while the action in the place would not be so specifically linked to its location.

In processional drama, the pageant wagons would be the areas for localised action – the equivalent of scaffolds in a static performance. The place could be a clearly limited central area, or simply the green or street. While some Mystery plays were processional, it is possible that N-Town provides us with a play text intended for static place-and-scaffold playing. If this is the case it would mean that the scaffolds would have been arranged around a delimited acting area in a manner similar to continental practice. At Mons for example, at a performance of a *Passion* in 1501, there were as many as seventy locations. The possibility of static performance would allow for the use of simultaneous staging, offering a more complex kind of dramatic effect. This idea of simultaneous action is found to a limited extent in the York Cycle, with coming and going between wagons in certain plays.[2]

More elaborate forms of such action were possible in place-and-scaffold playing, where the audience could see the links being made between different activities in a number of locations and would be able to move from one location of action to another, since they were not fixed to any specific seating arrangements. The conventions which are explored here in relation to the Morality plays have a relevance also to the consideration of the Mystery plays. The stage traditions are directly linked and share many features, such as for example the appearance and behaviour of stage devils, the use of Hell Mouth, the depiction of Heaven and so on.

Place-and-scaffold playing, in an outdoor setting, is best understood in relation to Morality plays by examining the large-scale spectacular Morality play *The Castle of Perseverance*, a play found in the Macro Manuscript. This is a collection of plays of East Anglian provenance, attesting to the strength of dramatic activity in this area. We are told something of the visual impact of this play by the details given in the diagram accompanying it. The colourful costumes may have had an allegorical significance; Peace wore black, Truth green, Mercy white and Righteousness red. The costuming directions for the actor playing the devil, Belyal, demonstrate the lengths these players would go to to mount a spectacle:

> And he that schal pley Belyal loke that he have gunnepowdyr brennynge in pypys in hys handys and in hys erys and in hys ars whanne he gothe to batayle.

The staging information contained in the famous diagram which accompanies the play *The Castle of Perseverance* on folio 191v. is worthy of a good deal of attention. Its main features are a castle, a ditch and several scaffolds. The castle is drawn as a single tower, with a bed beneath. There is also a cupboard for Avarice at the foot of this bed. The ditch surrounds the castle and we are told that it contains water. However, if a ditch cannot be made an alternative construction is suggested in the form of a fence or barricade. There are five scaffolds – God in the East, Flesh in the South, World in the West, Belyal in the North and Avarice or Covetousness at North-East.

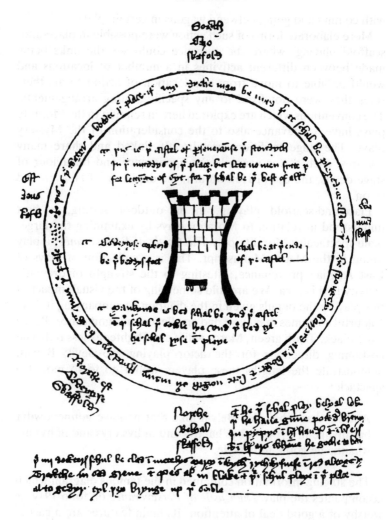

In the play the malefactors open the action, each one boasting from his respective scaffold. Various attempts are then made to tempt Mankind (Humanum Genus), who has both a Good and a Bad Angel. Backbiter persuades Mankind to join him at Avarice's scaffold where he invites the other six Deadly Sins to join him. The action is then centred on this scaffold. The Good Angel, probably centrally located, begs for help from Confession and Penitence. Mankind is lanced by Penitence and descends the scaffold to be absolved by Confession. He then enters the Castle of Perseverance and is defended within by the Seven Virtues.

The next movement is the central action of the play, the assault on the castle by the vices to retrieve Mankind. The Good and Bad Angels observe the scene. Eventually the siege is thwarted by the virtues throwing roses onto the vices to repel them. However, Avarice tempts Mankind to leave the Castle with the offer of money and power. At this point Death comes, in his traditional guise, and strikes at Mankind's heart. His last words are to cry for Mercy as the World's boy, I-Wot-Nevere-Whoo, dumps his body to get his riches. The Soul, carried off to Hell by the Bad Angel, is retrieved by the intercession of Mercy on his behalf and after the debate of the Four Daughters of God, Mercy, Truth, Justice and Peace, the Soul enters Heaven.

As we turn from the story line to the dramatic spectacle we should reflect that in narrative, space can only be transmitted by verbal means and it is therefore a relatively simple phenomenon. In the theatre, however, space is complex and there are several levels on it which can be viewed.[3] The broadest category, Theatre Space, is concerned with the architectural design of the theatre – the nature of the building in which the drama will take place. Theatre Space is an overview in historical terms while Stage Space, which is concerned with scenography, stage and set design – the use of scenery, properties, decor and setting – encompasses semi-fixed features. Finally, Dramatic Space, which covers the spatial concerns of individual plays and dramatists, deals with dynamic features, since it entails the mechanism of space, from one moment to the next as well as the relations linking space to other aspects of performance. The diagram which accompanies *The Castle of Perseverance* provides preliminary information about fixed or semi-fixed stage features, while the reconstruction of the stage action concerns features of dramatic space.

Interestingly, the main studies of the *Castle* diagram already described seem to conflict as to whether it concerns fixed or semi-fixed features. Richard Southern, for example, treats the diagram as a document relating to Theatre Space, whereas Natalie Crohn Schmitt considers it at the level of Stage Space. The drawing accompanying *The Castle of Perseverance* is apparently in the same hand as the play. It indicates a roughly circular playing area and five scaffolds. Southern's elaboration of the drawing, published in

1957 as a reconstruction of the Medieval Theatre in the Round,[4] came to be accepted as fact, offering a tidy explanation of the diagram and other evidence in tune with the theatrical interests of the 1950s. Southern argues that the diagram and play provide evidence of a large-scale professional theatre pre-dating the Eliza-bethan playhouses, and basing itself on aesthetic principles akin to the 'epic' theatre of the twentieth century. Contrary arguments have now been articulated and should be considered. Southern constructs the following staging arrangements. The audience stood or sat within the 'place', a theatrical term here meaning the area within the circle. The ring of water or bars was to keep out spectators unless they had paid. The scaffolds were inside the ring, inside the ditch, since the actors move freely between scaffold and place, and the actors also played in the place.

It is clear from the Banns, according to Southern, that a travelling company acted the play on tour and at each site a green would be found for the place of performance. Here the ditch would be dug or the place barred about. The ditch must have been 10 feet wide and 5 feet deep and the earth from the ditch formed a hill on which people could sit. The size of the circle would be about 110 feet across. The audience stood or sat on the grass but were not allowed into the central area, and Southern suggests that ushers were present to ensure that this part of the green remained clear for the actors.

Southern uses a number of pieces of supporting evidence to supplement the stage plan. These include the existence of earthworks in Cornwall, of the dimensions he specifies, where we know that plays were staged. These plan-an-guare, examples of which survive at St Just and Perranporth, are recorded also by Cornish antiquaries as places where the Cornish Passion plays were staged before 1600. He also refers to a miniature painting of a saint's martyrdom, *The Martyrdom of St Apollonia*, by the artist Fouquet, which he claims shows the martydom being staged in an arena like the one he claims was used for *The Castle of Perseverance*.[5]

Critics of Southern's hypothesis have attacked it from various directions.[6] The main area for dispute concerns the interpretation of the instructions between the two circular lines which mark the ditch and the positioning of the scaffolds. Around the ditch it says: 'This is the watyr a-bowte the place, if any dyche may be mad ther it schal be pleyed, or ellys that it be strongly barryd al abowt, and lete nowth ovyr many stytelerys be wyth-inne the plase.'[7] Southern places his ditches or stakes around the place, the scaffolds and the audience in order to construct his self-contained theatre, which would be professional and had a paying audience, who could enter by a single entrance over the ditch. The diagram clearly shows, however, the scaffolds outside the ditch, and if we are to accept Southern's plan we must also accept a less than literal view of the diagram.

Natalie Crohn Schmitt argues that the stage diagram, far from being the drawing of a theatre structure, is a set design and that the ditch in the drawing is not a trench round the outside of a theatre, but merely a moat round the castle, a conjecture which fits the drawing better and which eliminates the problems which arise concerning the construction of Southern's theatre. In Southern's view the water surrounds the place – but it also necessarily surrounds the mounds and scaffolds. In Schmitt's view the water surrounds not the whole playing area or place, but only that part of it which immediately surrounds the castle. Schmitt and others maintain that their interpretation of the sketch is more literal, in placing ditch and scaffolds in proper relation to each other.

This arrangement would dispense with the need for massive earthworks, and it is supported by archaeological findings. The discovery of East Anglian Game Places, such as that at Walsham le Willows,[8] and contemporary accounts of these places suggest what Southern found impossible to contemplate. Southern thought it was impossible for a ditch to separate the bank and the audience from the central platea, but this was clearly the case at Walsham le Willows in the neighbourhood where the *Castle* manuscript is known to have circulated. Here, a stone wall was placed within the earthworks, separating the mound from the central area of the platea, a configuration consistent with the textual and stage plan evidence.

If Southern's reconstruction is correct, the most far-reaching consequence of its findings is the change in viewpoint with regard to the professional stage and its origins. J. R. Elliot, an advocate of Southern's view, acknowledges the change it has instituted:

> The rediscovery of the Medieval stage has already had important
> consequences on our understanding of the whole course of
> English theatrical history. . . . Far from springing full-blown
> from the mind of James Burbage in 1576, the Elizabethan public
> theatre, in its design and stage craft, shows a clear ancestry
> reaching back to the medieval rounds and playing-places.[9]

This view of the medieval stage accepts the notion of the importance
of medieval drama, largely because of Southern's claim for a
professional theatre of considerable scale, pre-dating the Elizabethan public theatre.

The alternative interpretation of the diagram does not have a
bearing on architectural aspects of the theatre, but concerns rather
the second level of set design and stage plan. This view would not
give the Theatre-in-the-Round the status of architectural ancestor
to the Elizabethan Playhouse. However, a set design of the type
posited by Schmitt is clearly worthy of exploration in terms of its
dramatic potential.

The audience relationship to actors would operate rather differently in this type of theatre. While the circularity of space would
encompass the action, marked by the raised scaffolds, within this
area the space would not be homogeneously for use by all, actors
and audience, in all places. Whereas some areas would be shared,
others would be preserved exclusively for the stage action. This
division of space offers a rather more complex picture of actor–
audience relations. In some areas the intimacy of action observed
at close quarters, and even involving the audience, would operate,
whereas in other parts of the location the action would be offered
at more of a distance and with a definite barrier between the
groupings. The separation of outer and inner ring, the absence of
a mound which would allow the audience greater proximity to the
scaffold action (which would be observed therefore from a ground
level rather than almost on a horizontal level), are features which
significantly alter the dramatic groupings of the play from those
possible in Southern's type of theatre.

In this dramatic setting there is a degree of flexibility which can
be exploited to develop the dramatic range of the performance.
This staging would also have a potential for encouraging the use
of different areas to present visually significant groupings and give
prominence to several centres of action. Entrances and exits could

be effected from the area between the scaffolds, or almost imperceptibly by merging with the audience in the outer ring of the place. For crossings from the outer ring to the inner ring and vice versa we would have to assume a bridge across the moat, which is not shown on the stage plan, in the same way that Southern has to assume an entrance in his outer ditch.

Space is not only the static, the physical space made up of the playing area and spectators' area, but it is also dramatic space, the third level mentioned earlier, the dynamic spatial aspect of dramatic action, the constantly changing cluster of relations among actors, props and sets, the patterns of space relations throughout the play.

Dramatic space often coincides with the playing area itself, that is, what we see is the total dramatic space. This is known as mimetic space. But dramatists have a repertory of various strategies at their disposal to make the use of space and reference to space flexible. Whereas mimetic space is that which is visible and usually corresponds with the playing area itself, diegetic space depends on discourse only and is space which exists through description. When dramatic discourse refers to non-visible, diegetic space its function is to replace space verbally. This function can be seen in *Ane Satire of the Thrie Estaitis*, for example, when Placebo enquires as to the whereabouts of Solace and Wantonnes replies:

> I left Solace, that same greit loun,
> Drinkand into the burrows toun:
> It will cost him halfe of ane croun,
> Althocht he had na mair.
>
> (ll. 126–9)

The space here is not visible and the playing area has been extended by reference, by verbal means. This play is of a later date than *The Castle of Perseverance* and in it there is an interplay between the two types of dramatic space, mimetic and diegetic space. This kind of interplay is very prevalent in Elizabethan and Shakespearean drama.

In *The Castle of Perseverance* locations outside the visible playing area are not referred to. The play world and the world visible to the audience, or the real world, are one and the same and there seems to be nothing which exists outside this. Even the vaunting speech of the World, listing places where he has dominion, encompasses these places within the sphere of the play space, bringing them within it, rather than referring out to them (ll. 170–3).

There is no diegetic space in this play. When reference is made to space in the dialogue it is to focus our attention on mimetic space. The play, of course, uses a multiplicity of locations within the arena, so reference is to focus or anchor the use of different locations. For example, Confessio indicates a movement in location as he and Humanum Genus move toward the castle in the centre of the platea.

> To swyche a place I schal the kenne
> Ther thou mayst dwelle wythoutyn dystaunsce
> And alwey kepe the fro synne,
> Into the Castel of Perseveraunce.
> (ll. 1551–4)

To which Mankind replies that the castle is 'here but at honde' (ll. 1565–6).

The space used in *The Castle of Perseverance*, through its all-encompassing nature, represents the whole world. The audience is included in this world, which is bounded by the major outer scaffolds of World, Flesh, Devil, God and Covetousness (as primary sin). Yet, because there is no outer boundary, they and the action which proceeds in the place are not cut off from the real world, the world outside the play world, which blurs almost imperceptibly with the all-inclusive play space. This is a feature which allows a complex relationship between audience and actors, who are at any moment separate and yet the same, and between play space's entire world and the world of reality to be communicated.

Accompanying this feature of all-inclusiveness is the auto-reflexive nature of reference to space, where the actions performed in space and movements from one space to another are not only visible but are pointed out by the speakers.

The Castle of Perseverance essentially takes place, not in one acting area, but in a number of areas which have very specific spatial relationships to each other, which are established as part of the thematic action. In the arena there would be different kinds

of action taking place in different kinds of space. In some areas
the audience would be present while in other areas they would be
separated from the action, only able to watch from outside its
bounds. The arena as a whole would not, however, be cut off
from the everyday world although there would not be equally
open access for the audience in all areas.

The first speech of Mankind is usually described as a 'walking
and wending speech',[10] since each stanza seems to be delivered in
front of consecutive scaffolds surrounding the platea. In Southern's
arena, Mankind begins in the centre of the platea and moves out
towards the scaffolds. The alternative staging set, with the more
centralised moat, leaves two possibilities for staging the speech.
The first possibility is that Mankind is already located in the middle
of the playing area before the speech, in which case he will need
to cross the ditch or moat at some point. The second possibility is
that Mankind begins his speech in the outer area. For once the
barrier of the outer ditch is removed, as representative of mankind,
he could simply emerge from the audience, in much the way that
Everyman first appears. Death points out Everyman, presumably
from among the crowd:

> Lo, yonder I see Everyman walking.
> Full little he thinketh on my coming;
> (ll. 80–1)

However, the figure in *The Castle of Perseverance* is not pointed
out, but he tells us himself that 'I walke, I wende' (l. 227).

It would seem fully appropriate dramatically for Mankind to
begin as a lone figure in the middle area, as he contemplates and
attempts to make sense of his place in the world. His connection
with the rest of humanity is made clear, while his isolation from
them is highlighted: each man, though one of many, stands alone.
He may have circled the inner, rather than the outer, area to
deliver the speech. The text gives no clear indication of where he
begins his speech, but if he does begin in the inner area, his
reference to a ditch is the point at which he crosses over to the
outer area at the instigation of the Bad Angel (ll. 436–7).

The moat appears to be used to mark the transition from
confronting the Good and Bad Angels alone to coming into a
heavily peopled world in which Mankind's closeness to the crowd

links him to their situation. The inner and outer area of the platea are thus used both to link us with the action in a full and intimate involvement and to make us stand back and reflect on the action and its implications for the individual.

The central dramatic event of the play is the assault of the vices upon the castle. It is variously described as the Castle of Virtue, the Castle of Good Perseverance and the Castle of Goodness. The allegorical significance of the space in this central area need not then worry us, as we are told how to understand this space. The Castle of Goodness does not retain this significance throughout and the tracing of the action to some degree traces the fortune of this structure.

Edgar T. Schell has talked of the imitation of life's pilgrimage in *The Castle of Perseverance*.[11] Mankind's opening speech of walking and wending, already noted, is one of a number of such speeches which are spoken on the move and which indicate the circumambulation of the outer platea, marking the arrival at each of the scaffolds in turn. The process of linking changes in thematic action with changes in location presents in visible form what John Lyons terms the 'spatialisation of time'.[12] With a mobile audience, able to move with the actors to follow the action, the changes in location which apply to the characters will also apply to the audience and they are thus much more fully and directly implicated in the events than a static audience.

The uses of the journey motif and of other verbs which mark the process of change from one state to another are not usually regarded as metaphorical, and yet these are a reflection of this expression of time in spatial terms. The points in the play when Mankind reflects on his age and his changing physical state must be related to this notion of journeying and the resulting alteration in his state is found marked by changes in location.

The play is marked by a series of peripeteias. The first of these peripeteias comes when Confession (Confessio) and Penitence (Penitencia) come to the calling of Mankind's Good Angel. A modern audience may perhaps regard these as contrived. The scene marks a sudden tranformation of Mankind which is brought about, not by a gradual soul searching, but by a sudden and quite dramatic piece of thematic action, which forms a border-crossing, leading to the reintroduction of Mankind over the moat to the central area beneath the castle.

The thematic account of the action may help to explain its appeal within a theatre concerned to represent human experience in spatial terms. Interestingly, the moat seems to play a vital part in this boundary-crossing, for as Penance lances Mankind's heart he tells us:

> Wyth poynt of penaunce I schal hym prene
> Mans pride for to felle.
> Wyth this launce I schal hym lene
> I-wys a drope of mercy welle.
>
> (ll. 1382–5)

The well of mercy in this play is surely the water of the moat into which Penance dips the point of his lance before striking at the heart of Mankind. We know that the action takes place near the Castle of Perseverance, as the subsequent movement to it is effected very quickly. In one speech Confession (Confessio) says that he will send 'to yone castel' (l. 1559), using the pronoun 'yone', whereas in the following speech Mankind replies that the castle is 'but here at honde' (l. 1565), suggesting that the castle is very close.

We must conclude that the references indicate a differentiated space – a here and there which are fairly close in distance but separate and distinct. Later, the Good Angel tells Mankind to hurry to 'yone precyouse place', again suggesting a space in some way at a remove. We must see the change in Mankind in full, then, as the whole sequence of this movement, initiated by the sudden and dramatic change of heart but not fully effected until the movement has been completed. The change effected remains striking and marked but follows a progress which is mapped out by the movements in space. Both departure (the point of penance) and arrival (coming to the castle) are achievements over an interval of time.

The play develops this technique in which time is spatialised and the action thus realised should not be regarded simply as sudden and unmotivated. It must be seen in relation to the potential of the spatial possibilities of theatrical presentation to map out an account of experience. The suddenness of the piercing of man's heart by penance cannot be regarded in isolation, as it is part of a wider action.

The siege sequence is the part of the play in which the largest number of protagonists are massed within the space and the spatial relationships are therefore complex and crucial.

There are numerous references to water in this sequence of events, which support the notion that the moat around the central area marked a divide of locations. We must note Flesh's (Caro) remark that he uses shot and sling to cause the castle to fall crashing down into the water (ll. 1953–5), and the action of Sloth (Accidia), who, carrying a spade in conventional manner, proceeds to 'delve' in a 'dyche' containing 'watyr of grace' (ll. 2343–8).

The action of the siege as a whole suggests that, while the vices surround the moat, they do not pass it. If they had already crossed over there would be little dramatic impact in the activity of Sloth, who was trying to dig a channel through the moat to dry out this barrier to their access:

> Ye schulyn com ryth i-nowe
> Be this dyche drye, be bankys brede
>   (ll. 2347–8)

Sloth is therefore digging not only to spill the waters of mercy but also so that the vices can cross into the inner location. Busyness (Solicitudo) further explains:

> Therfor he makyth this dyke drye
> To puttyn Mankynde to dystresse.
> He makyth dedly synne a redy weye
> Into the Castel of Goodnesse.
>   (ll. 2369–72)

This leaves no doubt as to why this piece of action has been included. While the fighting in the siege does involve physical contact, it is of a kind which could be enacted across a divide such as a moat. Missiles are launched from either side of the ditch to land on the enemy at the other side, lances are used to span the distance and the atmosphere of conflict is increased by banners flying above. Ironically the siege is at an end with Sloth's cry that someone 'ley on watyr!'. The tempo of the play changes at this point as the technique to recover Mankind changes.

Covetousness begins with a plea to Mankind across the divide, encouraging him to regard him as his 'best friend' and with a series of mocking questions tries to get Mankind to reconsider his position. The address is intercepted by Generosity (Largitas), who answers in an attempt to fend off the threat. However, Covetousness' imprecations point to a welcoming space 'here' where Covetousness is, designed to encourage Mankind into intimate conversation, which can of course, only take place when both are near at hand. The coaxing specifies an exact response – that Mankind should reach out and touch his hand (l. 2494) and the closing of the gulf between the two figures is imaged in spatial terms across the physical divide separating them.

The change of speaker shows the Covetousness' technique is starting to have success. Mankind's series of bewildered questions are based on spatial concerns and point to some distant elsewhere and the notion of the journey returns – ('wey', 'wende') (ll. 2498 ff.).

These concerns turn immediately to the process of ageing, which closely links time and space in the play's frame of reference as Mankind's own body is focused upon as an object and he is anatomised in physical terms (ll. 2500 ff.).

After Mankind has forsaken the castle, each of the Virtues speaks in turn, exonerating herself from blame and explaining that Mankind has free will to do as he wishes. Possibly, the Virtues move out from the castle when making these excuses and leave it empty of goodness, as they move forward in explanation to the audience. Their part is played and they leave the scene either by walking away from the castle or by concealing themselves. In either case, their presence and influence no longer exist. The snaring of Mankind continues, however, as Covetousness plays out the scene of intimacy with Mankind, in striking contrast to the public display which took place in the siege.

Mankind turns his attention to his companion and asks for worldly wealth. He links the present to an imminent future fate by the phrase 'or that I dey' (l. 2747). Covetousness gladly obliges by giving his companion 'a thousand marke' (l. 2749).

It has been suggested that Covetousness gets the money from his cupboard in the central area under the platea. But all the indications are that the pair are moving away from the castle and not towards it at this point. There remains, however, the need to explain what is meant by 'Covetous' copbord' marked on the stage

plan. After Mankind has buried his money at some location close
to Covetousness' scaffold he asks for a castle of his own:

> Now wolde I haue castel wallys,
> Stronge stedys and styf in stallys.
> Wyth hey holtys and hey hallys,
> Coveytyse, thou must me sese.
>
> (ll. 2771–4)

It would seem likely that at this point Covetousness fixes on the
castle in the middle of the place as he replies: 'Al schalt thou haue
al redy, lo' (l. 2775), since he needs to obtain a castle which does
not have an incumbent tenant, as the scaffolds in the outer area
have. The pair move again from his scaffold and he tells him to
take 'al this good', as Mankind establishes his base in this central
castle. The cupboard then can store his covetously gained goods
in the way that a painting by Hieronymous Bosch shows a miser
using his cupboard.[13]

This relocates the action once again in the central area, but with
a strikingly different function for this castle. Through Mankind
the dominion of the world has stretched its confines into the
one area which previously provided a safe haven. The growing
physicality and materiality of the dialogue is accompanied by this
transformation of the castle from that of a spiritual stronghold to
one which is part of the material possessions of Mankind. It would
be an appropriate use of the castle, in the light of Mankind's
treatment of the Virtues who had brought him into their tower,
for as Covetousness says, everything he had has been obtained 'in
synful slo' by extorting it from his neighbours (ll. 2779–80).

Later in the play Mankind reacts to the coming of death with a
vivid evocation of its physical effects, recording man's increasing
years and decreasing vigour. The entry of the enigmatic I-Wot-
Nevere-Whoo into the action further extends the death scene, as
Mankind dies in the knowledge that his worldly possessions will
profit not his heirs, but someone who means nothing to him. This
scene too, like the peripeteia when Penance comes to Mankind,
is developed at some length with a clearly defined departure and
arrival point. The arrival point here comes with further action
involving the moat. In the Banns we are told that:

. . . Deth comyth foul dolfully and loggyth hym in a lake
(l. 99)

This line is not accounted for by Southern. In the play itself, however, the World's boy threatens:

In-to a lake I schal hym lyfte.
(l. 2936)

This threat is carried out, as immediately afterwards the conversation guides us to the stage action – the boy tries to lift Mankind, who objects by insisting that he is not dead yet:

GARCIO: Whou faryst, Mankynde? Art thou ded?
Be Goddys body, so I wene.
He is hevyer thanne any led.
I wolde he were gravyn vndyr grene.

HUM. GEN: A-byde, I breyd uppe wyth myn hed.
(ll. 2944–8)

The image is one of Mankind being dragged untimely from his deathbed towards the moat surrounding the castle.

If the moat is the water of mercy, a further development of the thematic action is that Mankind's last word alive is to call for Mercy. By an ironic twist, the callous Garcio figure should, unintentionally, while helping himself to Mankind's worldly goods, be helping Mankind to the source of his salvation. The later stages of the play further associate mercy with water:

Whanne man crieth mercy, and wyl not ses,
Mercy schal be hys waschynge-well:
(ll. 3168–9)

These lines gain in resonance when the action of the rest of the play is considered.

By looking at theatrical space and the ways it is indicated in this Morality play we have highlighted the importance of thematic action rather than the rising pattern of traditional plot analysis. The use of a thematic action allows the dramatist to link the audience to the chief protagonist in a meaningful and intimate way, which will involve them emotionally, not only with his fate, but with their own, and at the same time enables them to stand back, reflect and consider the 'mapping out' which has taken place in this mappemundi arena.

8
Audience and Performance

The Morality play and Interlude drama of the late medieval and early Tudor period is sometimes regarded as a single phenomenon, including humanist debates, farces, Morality plays and classical university dramas. Clearly the interconnectedness of these dramatic forms in this period and the cross-fertilisation of ideas from one form to another are important but there is a traceable difference between popular and elite traditions, both in the content of the entertainment and in method of staging.

The elaborate and costly medium of 'coterie' theatre had a tradition of highly decorative sets, scenic machinery and an impulse towards the social recreation of an audience drawn from the nobility. These non-popular dramas associated with the court, noble household or Inns of Court often relied on boy players or amateurs who never travelled outside their own households. Sets could be elaborate as they were not required to be movable. Similarly plays which needed large numbers of players could be arranged as these plays were often designed for a specific important occasion and they needed to be suitably impressive.

Plays in the popular tradition were somewhat different. The popular moralities were designed for performance by itinerant adult players, who were liveried retainers of an aristocratic patron, but who travelled all over the country acting for gain. Their plays required simple staging so that they could move from one location to another. They needed to be flexible to meet varying conditions of performance and their troupes were of limited size, so their

127

plays had small casts or relied on extensive doubling. Whereas these popular players sometimes performed in the halls of the nobility, they did not rely on an elaborate hall-screen and gallery. This was the drama of the whole nation, which noble audiences also shared, but it was not exclusive in any way.

Mankind is one of the fifteenth-century plays which clearly belongs to a popular tradition of entertainment, having affinities with sermon literature of its time. It also borrows from folk culture, incorporating folk play elements into the Morality tradition and thereby extending its flexibility in this direction. The play would adapt equally well to production in an inn-yard or in a large room, such as a hall, possibly using a booth stage in either setting. A recent production by the Toronto-based players, the Poculi Ludique Societas, relied on just such an arrangement and proved how flexible the staging requirements can be.

Mankind is found in the same manuscript as *The Castle of Perseverance*, the manuscript known as the *Macro Plays*, but it is strikingly different from the *Castle* in its scale and tone. The cast consists of seven characters, compared to the thirty-six named parts in the *Castle*. The play has many internal references to East Anglia and is usually dated at around 1470. The play centres on the sin of Sloth and explores this sin in relation to inactivity, 'idle language', a form of Sloth, and despair leading to Suicide, the ultimate result of Slothfulness, from which the Mankind figure can only be saved by Mercy. The devil of the play, Titivillus, is particularly appropriate, as he is the recording demon who collects man's sinful thoughts and utterances.

This devil also appears in the Mystery plays, in the Towneley-Wakefield *Last Judgement Play*, where he has been armed by Satan with a cloak of invisibility, a net and a satchel, to assist him in his task. The author of *Mankind* depicts the demon in this same way. There is also a group of vices in the play, led by Mischief who provides a foil to the preaching of Mercy. The play is in many ways a battle of words as the styles of speaking of virtue and vice are contrasted. Words are seen as of equal value to deeds, and while some may find the explicitness of some of the language shocking, it gives a seductively comical edge to the play. Other features which would appeal to a popular audience are the folk play elements and the depiction of the protagonist, Mankind, as a simple farmer.

Episodes in *Mankind* which are akin to the Mummers' plays are Mischief's offer to cure Nowadays' headwound by chopping off his head. This is akin to the Cure of the Mummer's doctor in the resurrection scenes of the plays. The collection which is taken is akin to the quete of the ritual plays. Titivillus' introduction of himself is like the introduction of characters in Mummers' plays. The references to his large head call to mind Beelzebub in the folk plays, and finally, the call for room is traditional to folk plays.[1]

The atmosphere of the play, with its scatological imagery and ribaldry, marks the play as decidedly popular in approach. The matter is far from elevated. The protagonist as a farmer, a man who digs and delves, is anchored by several figurative analogues. He is associated with a spade, a plot and corn and therefore has associations with both Adam and Cain: the biblical links are further expanded by the fact that the play continually refers to life as a series of tests, like those met by Job.

There is a great deal of violent action in the play, much of which is comic in effect. The play thus contains the extremes of bad language and slapstick action which are associated with popular comedy. The audience is encouraged, by a process of habituation, to see threats associated with the vices as comical posturing. When Mischief enters the play he tells us he has come to make game, and when Mercy is challenged by the vices' slapstick and verbal play the audience laughs with the vice figure. In the same way, when the violent action of the scene in which Mankind fends off the vices with his spade gives way to the comic lament of Mischief as mere sotte, the danger is diffused and the audience is encouraged to treat the vices lightly as comedy rather than threat. Another point to mention about the lament is that at the end of the play another lament is made – this time by Mercy. This may suggest some kind of structural paralleling or the pairing of Mercy and Mischief for comparison.

The audience response becomes crucial at Mankind's temptation. Following the lament Mischief changes role – from mére sotte to the doctor,[2] who is usually called upon by the lamenter to cure the victim. This role change could be explained as being necessary because of the limited number of actors, which would make the enactment of the Mummers' play proper impossible, but it is also rather unsettling since the transition breaks the convention and the stepping out of and between roles is likely to confuse.

What is interesting about this passage is the way that one role merges into another, so that the normally clear demarcation of character type and associated action becomes blurred, confused and unsettled. Thus, we may comment that the passage seems to be working by making gradual shifts from one kind of action to another, from one role to another, leaving the audience uncertain about the identity of speakers and the actions which can be expected of them.

One method which can be used to trace this process is to consider that the speaking of language is not merely the conveying of content, but is a form of doing in its own right,[3] promising, warning, lamenting, querying and so on. Such an approach will shape the discussion here. Mischief begins, following Mankind's exit:

> Alas, alas! that ever I was wrought!
> Alas! the while I [am] worse than nought!
> Sithen I was here, by Him that me bought!
> I am utterly undone!

> (ll. 411–15)

Looking at the negation in the passage, it should be noted that the word 'undone' takes the negative particle into the form of the word; the adjective 'worse' and the noun 'nought' all add to the negativeness of the passage. The broken nature of the first two sentences (the first line has no syntactic opening and the second omits its verb) and the expletives add to the sense of regret in the statements. These opening statements establish Mischief's responsibility and he goes on to blame himself for the beating which the vices have received. The whole speech is directed at the audience and this is made still clearer when Mischief makes a query 'Will ye list?'. This is a call for a response from the audience, an attempt to involve them. It resembles present-day pantomime methods in the directness of its address. The speech merges into role-playing as the vices enter, with Mischief's invitation ('veni, veni – Come hither') as comforter of the vices. Here the audience are being spoken to by extra-dramatic address, a mode which places them in a position of separateness from Mankind and which offers them special insights into the events taking place. This role-playing recalls Mischief's earlier remark 'I am come hither to make you game' and in this speech again Mischief mentions 'the game' (l. 418). A further change of role occurs within a single speech. The speech opens in the role of mere sotte:

> Lady, help! silly darling! veni, veni!
> (l. 432)

but it continues:

> I shall helpe thee of thy pain;
> I shall smite off thy head, and set it on again
> (ll. 433–4)

In the first line Mercy resembles the Mummers' Doctor in his avowal to 'cure', but there is the hint of a threat in the second line, akin to that of the swordplay. Thus Mischief conflates the two roles: the doctor, a quack of course ('I am the Doctor and I cure all ills / Only gullup my portions and swallow my pills') and the swordsman ('We have all concluded to cut off your head').[4]

The transition from mere sotte is made by two acts of affirmation and the resolution to help rather than comfort. The mere suggestion of such drastic action is enough to act as a cure. Mischief 'helps' by producing the effect of threatening them out of their pain. This role-playing, involving transitions from one kind of role to another, becomes increasingly unsettling, since the figure of Mischief gains darker and darker overtones, and what at first seems like concern turns to aggression towards his fellow vices. While an audience may laugh, and the threat is soon dispersed, the episode does give a sense that there are disquieting features involved in these characters. There is some doubt whether this is such a harmless game – but then the rapid movement into the next episode disperses such fears.

The technique used by the dramatist can be illuminated by a consideration of the views of a twentieth-century literary theorist, Mikhail Bakhtin, whose notion of 'carnival' is well illustrated by the dramatic method in *Mankind*.[5] The carnival spirit is not an art form, as all participate in the creation, neither is it reductive like modern satire, as the creators are also mocked by it. Carnival travesties, it inverts rank and exchanges roles, it makes sense of nonsense and nonsense of sense. It has an inside-out logic showing the arbitrariness of all norms and rules. Carnival expresses glee and shows the relativity of all things without fearing any judgement. It merges the individual into the collective and the result is the grotesque realism which can be seen in the scatology and ribaldry of *Mankind*, where those things which are usually considered unmentionable are highlighted as the essential processes: shitting, pissing, basic biological needs. Carnival is framed off from everyday life, as it is in this play world, so that the sense of relativity is kept in a safe place, at a distance which allows you to laugh fearlessly. It can thus be seen as a method of social control, offering release, without challenging the norms and the values of society. Yet carnival is always potentially dangerous, because no frame is ever totally secure. It is this knife edge that is walked by the *Mankind* dramatist – and by the audience who are actively and creatively involved in this dangerous game.

Violent action in this game frame, like in the folk play, is both hilarious and threatening. New Guise remarks, 'Ye shall not chop my jewels, and I may', and from this we know that even the most private bodily parts (the genitals) are threatened, in this supposed cure. No wonder each of the vices protests that he is cured (ll. 380–446)! These negatives ('I haue none harm', 'ye shall not chop my jewels') demonstrate to Mischief that there is considerable doubt in his ability to fulfil his claim. Thus his reaction reasserts this ability by the use of the modal 'can':

> I can chop it off, and make it again.
>
> (l. 444)

The modality of 'can' shows Mischief standing by his ability, though there is never any proof offered, since the vices are cured by the suggestion of his action. The vices, by claiming that there is no need for further help, avoid the possible consequences of further action, while allowing Mischief to maintain his claim 'I can'. They quickly change the subject of conversation. It is clear that the episode as a whole must have an unsettling effect on the audience, since the whole outcome is unfamiliar and uncertain, and, possibly, highly dangerous. It is because of such methods that in these instances in the play there is an uneasy tension between humour and disturbance, for the episode which at first seems to be a straightforward way to deflate Mankind's victory turns into a very 'uneasy' game. This usefully prepares the way for the entry of Titivillus, who also enters somewhat humorously but who also is a quizzical and rather ambivalent character. Humour merges almost imperceptibly into danger in the play for the audience, the privileged onlookers of all the action.

Before the devil appears various methods are used to increase tension. The vices form a huddle for a secret discussion when the audience can see them but not overhear their remarks and the suspense is increased by the flute-playing, and Titivillus' off-stage remark: 'I come with my legs under me'. This gnomic utterance has an effect akin to that of a remark commented upon by J. R Searle, in his book on speech acts:

> If a happily married man says, 'I promise that I will be faithful' to his wife, while the superficial effect of the statement is to reassure, the underlying effect is to unsettle the wife, since such a promise would only be made verbally if a hypothetical infidelity had already been contemplated by the husband.[6]

Similarly, 'I come with my legs under me' at first seems to be a reassurance that his appearance will, at least in this way, be normal: his legs will be where they ought to be. But such a reassurance suggests that this may not always be the case. That is why the propositional addition to the statement 'I come' makes the whole statement unsettling. It opens the way to the suggestions of the power and supernatural nature of Titivillus. The collection preceding Titivillus' entry is also used to build up suspense. The collection may have been a set piece, perhaps accompanied by virtuoso performances, such as the flute-playing, in order to show the troupe's range of entertainment skills for which an appreciative audience would be expected to pay. As the vices summon Titivillus, 'Come forth now your gatus', they warn the audience, 'Make space and beware', building up further the sense of expectation. Titivillus' first words on stage are full of associative echoes:

> Ego sum dominantium dominus and my name is Titivillus
> (l. 475)

The associations awakened here in the audience are to Deuteronomy 10.17 and Revelation 19.16, but most immediately to the

Medieval Drama

voice of God who on his first appearance in the Mystery plays begins 'Ego sum alpha et omega'.

'I am', is classificatory and in another time would glance towards the Cartesian 'cogito'. But the stance in the case of God in the Mystery plays is, moreover, that of declaring existence, and while Titivillus' remark is quizzical (as the latter half of the speech suggests), his pose is akin to this. The first half of the line is again the same kind of statement which is awesome and dangerous; the second half of the line undercuts it completely. After all the suspense and the opening half-line of Titivillus, this demon appears to be a tremendous anti-climax, the audience's fear being deflated into an uneasy laughter once again. The demon and his vices involve the audience in a series of in-jokes, mentioning particular people that the local Cambridge-area audience, where the play was performed, may have known personally. These may have even been people who were in the audience! The suggestion is made that these local people have a kinship with the vices, and the audience are thus allied to them by this shared laughter. Titivillus, for example, tells the vices to go and see where they could do any harm and to take William Fide (who may either be in the audience or known to them) if they need anyone else to help (ll. 502–3).

Titivillus was also known in popular literature as the Recording Demon, as the devil who listens for bad language, gossiping, frivolity and tittle tattle and collects these in a sack to record these sins and bring them before God to damn the sinner. The recording demon appears in popular sermon literature in this guise, most notably in a collection of sermons called *Jacob's Well*.[7] The relevance of this demon to the play *Mankind* is clear, as the play concerns slothful behaviour and the Mankind figure is led into this by means of the whispering of the demon and he then participates in the 'idle' language of the vices.

Titivillus' first speech of some length occurs at lines 522–40. After dismissing the vices he begins to reveal his plans, setting out his future intentions and actions as a preliminary to the Fall of Mankind (ll. 525 ff.).

The plan, its method of execution and its results are all set out:

Ever I go invisible – it is my jet –
And before his eye thus I will hang my net

To blench his sight;

(ll. 529–31)

The 'I' figure, performing all these future actions, bringing about the future downfall, is concentrated upon, so that in the following events we know who is responsible and whose achievements we are watching. Yet among all the promises and warnings with the 'I' figure dominating, there appear the following lines:

> To irk him of his labour I shall make a frame.
> This board shall be hid under the earth, privily;
> His spade shall enter, I hope, unreadily.

(ll. 532–4)

The passive form totally removes the agent of the action. After all the statements of 'I shall do something', this crucial piece of action in the plan has no agent in the surface structure. This seems to be deliberate, just as Titivillus' invisibility in the real action is deliberate. It appears here that the inanimate objects, the board and the spade, have taken over the initiative. This too will be how he wishes the real action to appear. In the line, 'His spade shall enter . . .', the spade is the active agent and it has an active verb attached to it – it enters – before the adverbial negative, which only negates after the action is syntactically complete. Alternative constructions could have made Mankind the agent, as he is when he attacks the vices ('with my spade I shall you ding') or an alternative negative could have preceded the verb. The syntax chosen adds to the sense that the agents of the actions are the inanimate objects conspiring against Mankind.

Thus, the syntax shows how Titivillus will achieve his aims, while we are made aware through the speech acts which stated his intentions, promises and boasts, that the achievement is his. It is at this point in the play that the complicity of the audience with evil forces is most evident and most crucial. Titivillus' requests for 'counsell' must be fulfilled for his plot (l. 539) to work and Mankind to Fall: 'And ever ye did, for me keep now your silence' (l. 590).

The position of omniscience of the audience here is very important: they can see Titivillus where Mankind cannot and, because of their position as confidante, they assume that the code used places them in the role of enlightened observer.

When Titivillus has begun his assault on Mankind the promises continue (ll. 556–8):

I promise you I have no lead on my heels.

Subsequently, he tells us what he has done in a series of boasts, taking pride in his achievement:

I-wis I am wonder-wise
I have sent him forth to shit lesings.
(ll. 566–9)

Promises and boasts continue to alternate until Titivillus finally leaves us with a bold acceptance of his achievement of Mankind's Fall, and a summary dismissal of his accomplices, the audience, 'for I have done my game' (ll. 606–7).

Theatrical satire is evident in the use of the board, which was presumably placed over the floor of the Hall or on the hard inn-yard floor, and in the antics of the supposedly invisible character, who is fully visible to the audience. The comedy conforms to the code to which the audience have gradually been habituated. Thus, the contradictions in the action of the play are geared towards this preferred code with which the audience are encouraged to comply. The active contradictions in the play involve the audience in a choice: whether or not to comply with the vices. The patterning of the action and the speech action by the vices attempts to direct their decision.

The play uses the audience's ability to identify with and to stand back from the Mankind figure in a topsy turvy carnival way. The usual enlightenment which comes from standing back and watching dispassionately the follies of the Mankind figure is put into a reversal. Instead, the speech and action of the vices offer a preferred reading (that sin is merely harmless joking), which is associated through the conventions attaching to the mode of extra-dramatic address, with insight.

The audience laugh at Mankind. In this very act, however, they have been duped as he has. For the play to be effective theologically, and for it to maintain the ideology dominant for the culture of its day, the play must show that preferred reading to have been aberrant, and a false insight. If the play does not effect this we must conclude that either it fails in its purpose or that it is a sham Morality, with subversive intentions. It is clear from the lament by Mercy that the playwright is gradually encouraging the association of direct address with the resumption of identity with Mankind. The risks involved are the risks of carnival, that order cannot be restored and the audience turned about. If successful, the audience have not just watched but will themselves have experienced directly the sinfulness they share with Mankind, and recognised it as aberrant. Much therefore hangs on the ending of the play.

There are strong structural parallels between the final scene and the opening one. Mercy has a long speech, interrupted by Mischief and the vices in a similar vein but a point of reversal is provided by the fact that it is Mercy who holds the rod, rather than one of the vices. The adverbial addition to the exclamation: 'Man unkind, wherever thou be!' broadens the reference of the speech to all mankind. As Mercy returns to the subject of Christ's Passion, which occupied so much of the first speech made by Mercy to the audience as mankind, there is a suggestive relinking of Mankind and the audience. Thus, the blame in the stanza could be seen to apply equally to them.

Because of the framework of direct address which is built into this speech, the final rhetorical questions have a double valence: they may in fact be questions directed, not to Mankind, but to the audience:

> Why art thou so uncurtess, so inconsiderate?
> (l. 754)

The suggestive possibilities of these modes of address, coupled with the topic of speech so reminiscent of Mercy's first speech, in which Mankind and audience were synonymous, if effectively conveyed could not fail to produce a changeover in the audience's role in the play. Once more they would identify with Mankind instead of seeing themselves as enlightened observers separate from his experience. When Mankind reaches that low point of slothfulness, Despair, and prepares (with the vices' help) to commit suicide, the audience can see the real harm which has been done by idle jokes.

At the end of the play Mankind recalls how 'Titivillus, that goeth invisible, hung his net before my eye'. His description of his fall is similar to the events which it has been suggested befall the audience. Those members of the audience who accepted the preferred reading of events offered by the vices, and associated this with enlightenment, were blinded to the fact that they too were imperceptibly tricked, and that far from their being separate from Mankind their experience was directly comparable.

The dramatic experience offered is tinged with danger, as the opportunity to recover the audience from the travesties of the vices hinges wholly on the playing of the last scene. But, by morally implicating them experientially through subversive laughter, the play leaves them no alternative but to face their own sinful natures head on. Thus, while we find order restored at the end of the play, the prime theatrical response may well be that of delight in the carnival energy, a response which celebrates the play world creation.

9
Signifying Practices

The religious drama of the medieval period may seem at first to a modern audience to be at some remove from the contemporary issues of its day, concerned rather with the universal and timeless. This would be an anachronistic view of medieval religious activity, for the Morality play was a form which could be used for ideological ends, to promote certain causes by dramatic means. In this sense it was a form ideally suited to political activity, firstly from within the Church and later looking outward to other spheres of influence. Writers of Morality plays were not merely apologists for established order; their work demonstrates a consciousness of the forces at work in the contemporary social scene and they were not afraid to speak out on issues of the day.

Everyman can be seen in precisely these terms, as an expression of the desire for reform from within the Church. It was a play to meet a crisis in its time, of highly topical content, and yet is regarded now as universal and timeless in quality. Indeed, this topicality is intrinsic to the structural balance of the play. A play with related concerns, produced at a similar time and under the influence of the same reforming movement is *Wisdom, who is Christ*, also known as *Mind, Will and Understanding*. The concern of this play is worldly political activity by the religious orders and the related contemporary phenomenon of defection from the monasteries. David Bevington has pointed out that the crux of the political point was the evil of the fifteenth-century practice of maintenance and the corruption which arose through it.[1] It

139

threatened civil authority as it had become a kind of legal protection racket. The parodic effects in the play are carried by the elaborate and lavish costumes, which acquire a new significance in this political perspective.

The full stage directions in the play show how its effects are to be achieved:

> Here entur six dysgysyde in the sute of Mynde, wyth rede berdys, and lyons rampaunt on here crestys, and yche a warder in hys honde; her mynstrallys, trumpes. Eche answere for hys name.

Mind plays the role of Maintenance and calls in his six retainers who 'wolde ber wp falsnes / And maynten yt at the best'. The costuming is complementary to the parodic ritual action, contributing to the broader meaning of the play. Mind, Will and Understanding, as clerics of newly acquired political power, are practised in the art of legal trickery. The six jurors who appear in the pageantry are described in some detail too, as their costumes are part of the signifying process.

> Here entrethe six jorours in a sute, gownyde, wyth hodys abowt her nekys, hattys of meyntenance thervpon, vyseryde dyuersly; . . .

Their visors or masks suggest the two faces of perjured jurors, while the hats were given by way of livery for maintenance.

Wisdom has an idealised ending suggesting the need for self-reform and in this the play reflects its allegiances to the religious writings which were its sources. This school of thought, akin to the Devotio Moderna, was a revolt against extreme asceticism, possibly because it believed an overemphasis on withdrawal from the world and extreme self-deprivation led to its opposite extreme, abuse and departure from monastic ideals. A balance between worldliness and the active life was to be sought, rejecting extremes in either direction, and finding an individual path through personal devotion to Christ's burning love, while accepting the Church's creed. Writers such as Richard Rolle, Walter Hilton, Henry Suso and St Bernard typify this approach.

It is easy to envisage how the Morality play could acquire a new impetus towards political issues in the social world of the Tudor court. Henry Medwall's play *Fulgens and Lucres*, though not a Morality, shows some of the signifying functions costuming acquired in this milieu. Again, Bevington's work on Tudor politics and drama gives us a lead.[2] The play was written against the background of an emerging new order of a humanist state in which the power and influence of the nobility were being challenged by an emerging intelligentsia of humanist thinkers, many of whom were churchmen or acolytes and who formed a nascent civil servant group, with influence over state affairs. In these terms the figures of Publius, the representative of the old order or baronial class, and Gaius, the new man, represent the different interest groups in this power struggle.

The difference between these two emerges much more strongly through their dress than through their discourse. According to the servant B, Publius spends large sums of money on his clothes, on fashionable striped stockings, a large codpiece, and short gowns which use up wastefully large amounts of cloth in the sleeves. We can envisage his dress as demonstrating to a contemporary audience decadent conspicuous consumption (ll. 695 ff., Part 1). Publius, so costumed, would contrast strikingly with the moderation of Gaius, their different attitudes to marriage visually displayed by the size of the codpieces, the one representing a view of marriage as carnal pleasure, the other as the means of lawful procreation.

Play on identity, in part through appearance and costuming, is one of the most notable features of the Tudor plays. A and B, who comment on this play's action and who some have regarded as merely comic relief, are not exempt from this. Their interchanges and their status in the drama provide us with a highly creative example of theatrical meta-language, which is the framing of a language, or, in the case of the theatre, a set of conventions, holding it up as an object in its own right to be commented upon. If there is any way in which language may achieve materiality it would be by means of meta-language. The explicit framing of language has a long-standing tradition in drama and there are two main forms which meta-language takes and two basic object-languages which may be highlighted: external and internal meta-language.[3]

External meta-language treats the conventions of the drama as the object. The commentary so provided serves to frame the theatrical context of the communication and the relationship of actor to audience. In *Fulgens and Lucres* the roles of the servants A and B straddle play world and reality, and thus their status is brought into question. A and B begin the play by mingling with the crowd of spectators and it is only when Cornelius addresses 'so many good fellows as been in this hall' that they come forward to serve. In their introduction to the play, F. S. Boas and A. W. Reed consider that 'the consequence of this intermingling of actors and spectators is an imperfect sense of dramatic objectivity'.[4] Yet the use of the characters A and B is really an extension of the traditional methods of medieval playwrights, including those of the Mystery plays where anachronisms in names, dress and dialogue are used to make the scriptural events depicted directly applicable to a contemporary audience. The method is one which foreshortens time and place, in the case of *Fulgens and Lucres* bringing Roman antiquity and the contemporary time of the audience together, since such separation is irrelevant *sub specie aeternis* in a medieval context.

It is worthwhile, with regard to uses of meta-language, to look at the dialogue of A and B both before and during their involvement in the mimetic action of the play. During the course of their initial dialogue they bring up the topic of the play which is to be performed, but they continually deny that it is anything to do with them – they have merely turned up to watch:

> A: For I thought verrily by your apparel
>   That ye hed been a player.
> B: Nay, never a dell!

> (Part 1, ll. 48–50)

Later, both A and B again deny their involvement in the play and protest that they are like any other member of the audience:

> A: For why? in this matter we have nought to do!

> (Part 1, l. 146)

It is only by Cornelius' direct invitation that first B and later A, become involved in the play proper, as if they were like any of the other revellers in the hall:

CORNELIUS: So many good fellows as [be] in this hall,
    And is there none, Sirs, among you all
    That will enterprise this geare?

                              (Part 1, ll. 354–6)

When B decides to take on the office, A, still retaining the pretence that they are ordinary observers, warns him:

A: Peace, let be!
  By God! Thou wilt destroy all the play.

to which B replies:

B: The play began never till now.

                     (Part 1, ll. 363–4, 366)

The ambiguity of A and B is crucial to their role in the entertainment and yet, according to William Dodd, in terms of meta-language if the speaker is not part of the fictive action then he or she cannot be seen as a dramatis persona and thus will have no more title than the spectator to unmask a convention.[5] Whether A or B have title to unmask a convention depends firstly on whether or not they are to be regarded as spectators or as actors. They seem to have a credible claim to both roles. A further consideration is whether or not their speech can be taken as within the sphere of interaction of the internal axis of the play or whether it is quite superfluous to its meaning and unity as such. For their discussion to be meta-linguistic its object must be the language of the play and not the play as a social convention. It is clear that if the two characters at the outset can be regarded as operating outside the sphere of the play, encoding the play as social convention and the passage from the everyday frame into the play frame rather than thematising theatrical conventions, they do not remain so.

At the opening of Part 2 of the play, with A and B firmly established in roles within the inner play world, B tells us that Cornelius has arranged for us to see a mumming and we are told by A what has happened in the play and that there were 'divers toys' mingled in the substance of the play to entertain people (Part 2, ll. 19–24), before the rest of the company returns. Clearly these are examples of external meta-language which thematise the play conventions. Interestingly, the very intermingling to which Boas and Reed took exception is the feature which provides an encoding of the play as social convention and which thematises the dramatic conventions, drawing social world into play world and expanding play world out to meet the social context, providing a role for the audience in the game without pretending that the game does not exist.

Changes of identity in the Morality plays and Interludes are marked by the stage action of changing dress. The action works as a kind of boundary marker between moral states. The related act of name-changing highlights some of the ways the flexibility of the Morality form can be seen to demonstrate changing beliefs and assumptions.

In *Mankind* the shift from virtue to sin is marked by a garment change, while the name of the protagonist remains the same, whereas in the later play, *Youth*, the shift to a different moral condition is marked by a name change (to Good Contrition) as well as a change of garments. Assuming a false name in the medieval plays is another common stage activity and the audience are informed of the deception. In *Doctrine, Occupation and Idleness*[6] the character Idleness tells his audience that he must change his name to Busyness (*Doctrine, Occupation and Idleness*, ll. 108–9). The audience's complicity is underlined and their moral involvement thereby achieved when they are asked to bear witness for what he says later in the play (ll. 130–1).

In *Magnyfycence* name-changing is one of the key parts of the action. Numerous aliases are set up, involving a large number of characters. The vices, however, do not inform the audience as to their real identities and the divergence between real and assumed identity emerges only through conversation, in which the audience are not directly addressed but are unacknowledged onlookers. After Fansy has already introduced himself as Largesse, Counterfeit Countenance enters and almost gives the game away. This is the first indication the audience has that Largesse is not who he says he is:

COUNTERFEIT C: What, Fansy, Fansy!
MAGNIFICENCE: Who is that that thus did cry?
   Methought he called 'Fansy'.

FANSY: It was a Fleming hight Hansy

(ll. 325–8)

The audience is no further enlightened than Magnyfycence until they overhear the conversation between the vices.

COUNTERFEIT C: But I say, keepest thou the old name still that thou had?

. . .

FANSY: Nay, nay, he hath changed his, and I have changed mine.

(ll. 516, 518)

The audience are eavesdroppers in this exchange, and it is only by this means that they too are not duped. The Tudor plays treat the audience very differently in this regard and the status of their involvement is closer to that of a modern audience. There is a shift away from using the assumption of false identity as a thematic action involving the audience in moral complicity, towards using the device to highlight the different states of knowledge between audience and protagonist. The comic possibilities of a character forgetting his assumed identity are played upon in *Ane Satire of the Thrie Estaitis*, by Sir David Lindsay. Here Falset forgets his alias when presented to the King and stands tongue-tied. When the King asks 'Sapience' why he forgot his own name the character tries to make the error fit his assumed identity:

> I am sa full of Sapience,
> That sumtyme I will tak ane trance:
> My spreit wes reft fra my bodie,
> Now heich abone the Trinitie.
>
> (ll. 874–7)

In the medieval period names had a sacred potency. Scholastic thinkers presented several views on this subject. Aquinas believed that names should agree with the nature of things as God-given, while Hugh of St Victor credits man's God-given reason with the naming of things. In medieval plays such as *The Castle of Perseverance*, the self-identification of a speaker by an act of naming gave the audience a clear and unequivocal notion of what quality would be demonstrated by this dramatis persona:

I hatte drery Dethe . . .
(l. 2790)

In Tudor plays the social aspects of holding a name become the chief focus of the identifying process, as the application of the Morality genre to political satire and affairs of state develops.

A far more man-centred approach to the question of naming and identity can be seen in, for example, *Mundus et Infans*, where the figure of Mankind appears under a series of aliases which mark the main transitions in his approach to life. When we observe a renaming in these plays the status of the name-giver and the procedural aspects of the act are clearly of some importance. In *Doctrine, Occupation and Idleness* the name-changing is preceded by a series of commitments demanded by Doctrine and made by Idleness using the form 'I will'. The ceremonial quality of the name change marks it as of a different order to the assumption of a false name by Idleness earlier in the play so that here we see the two procedures explicitly contrasted in one play. In *Ane Satire of the Thrie Estaitis* Lindsay turns the topical attack on the false-seeming of clerical garments into an extended rehearsal sequence in which the three vices, Flatterie, Falset and Dissait, assume clerical disguises and take the names of 'Devotion', 'Sapience' and 'Discretion' in a lively mock-baptism scene in which the normal procedural conditions are parodied. Lindsay thus uses this Morality convention to comment upon contemporary social malpractices.

This flexibility in approach to the act of naming demonstrates a gradual shift in the apprehension of the relationship between names and things. The interconnectedness of name and identity which is so apparent in the earlier medieval plays is replaced by a more fluid apprehension of the social, man-made nature of the connection, still based on a relation of resemblance, but in this case an outer similarity better fitted to the Morality play's adaptation to political and social ends. Shifts in discourse formation of this order are part of the historical process of a society undergoing transformation, and increasingly concerned with earthly power. This may be regarded as an epistemic way of explaining discourse, akin to the processes exposed by the French philosopher Michel Foucault in later periods.[7]

In the years of the Reformation, religious belief was a political issue, linked very closely to the wielding of earthly power: the changing discourse of the Morality play can only be understood when this context is fully appreciated. The fortunes of playwright John Bale give a clear account of the way that political fortunes vacillated at this time, according to the religious outlook of the monarch. Bale, an ardent Protestant, converted before England adopted state Protestantism, found favour under Chancellor Cromwell, but was forced into exile when Cromwell fell from grace. He was recalled from abroad in Edward VI's reign and eventually became a bishop. No sooner had the appointment been made than he was forced into exile again, on the accession of the Catholic Queen Mary. He returned to England once again under Elizabeth's reign. Bale was responsible for several developments of the Morality play form and his dramatic activities placed him in some danger at times.

10
Popular and Elite: the Legacy

Theatre historians have been at pains to trace the ancestry of the Elizabethan Playhouse and the thriving secular dramatic experience it offered to its audience. Various accounts of this ancestry have been proffered. Some have seen in the medieval arena theatre an ancestor to the circular structures of the Elizabethan Playhouse, adapted from the animal-baiting houses of contemporary London. Others have accounted for the apron stage and tiring house by perceiving its origins in the booth stage or in the pageant wagon, where the action could be staged on different levels. Still others have seen the drama of the banqueting hall, and particularly its use of screen, gallery and doors as exerting the dominant formative influence.[1]

We know that between 1497, the date of the first secular English comedy, Medwall's *Fulgens and Lucres*, and 1576, the date of the building of Burbage's Theatre in Shoreditch, the first Elizabethan Playhouse, there existed seventy plays which have come down to us in some form. Between these dates there was clearly a period of quite intense dramatic activity. A short account of the drama of this period will not only help to account for the dramatic experience of the Elizabethan stage, but will also prove that it is a period of experimentation, development and innovation worthy of attention for its own sake. While accepting that a knowledge of the Interludes can help in the understanding of the Elizabethan drama, it is intended that the concentration here will fall on encouraging the reader to appreciate and enjoy the drama of the

Interlude for itself, and not as some kind of prehistoric appendage to Shakespeare studies.

That the popular and courtly traditions were separate strands in the Interlude drama is clear. It is also clear that each influenced the other and that there was always a possibility of cross-fertilisation between traditions. Interludes of the sixteenth century are associated with a specific place of performance, the Tudor Great Hall. This would have had a raised dais at one end, tables down the two long sides and an open area in the centre of the floor, free for playing. At the lower end were the screens, which were three partitions having two doors, openings where servants could enter and exit to a passage way known as the entry, leading off to the kitchens. Above the screens there may have been a minstrels' gallery. The requirements for performance within this hall setting gradually became more complex as the century progressed. In the early sixteenth century the conditions of performance were simple, as the plays require just the open floor of the hall and the doors and screens, with props such as chairs and hand properties and possibly elaborate costumes.

In the sixteenth century doubling was a feature associated with the popular canon, for in the interests of economy it was wise to keep the number of adult travelling players in a troupe as small as possible. No such constraint was necessary in the case of amateur players who performed in the courtly or elite dramatic spectacles, which would be much more lavish and ostentatious displays. The effect of heavy doubling on the organisation and structure of the plays was a phenomenon peculiar to popular drama of this period, as David Bevington recounts in his book *From Mankind to Marlowe*.[2] No drama at any other time has ever been constructed around such a requirement: it is a decisive factor in the dramatic structures which emerge from this tradition.

In the early sixteenth century two writers with courtly connections, John Skelton and John Bale, both wrote plays with a popular impetus, borrowing elements from the traditions of native English drama. Skelton's *Magnyfycence* with its eighteen characters, clearly making use of the Morality tradition in its allegorical basis, can be performed by five actors, by means of careful doubling, but because of this need for doubling the good characters and the bad characters never meet.

The action takes place in the 'place', on the floor of the hall, an area which would contain both actors and audience. The crowded conditions, the intermingling of audience and performers and the torch-light conditions within the hall all contribute to an atmosphere which encourages a free and easy commerce between reality and the fictive; the players come into the natural space of the audience, rather than the audience going to a special theatre building with the specific purpose of seeing a play. There is an intimacy and spontaneity in the relationship between performers and their audience. In part this spontaneity is deliberately created by directly addressing the audience in a blunt and forthright manner, a manner borrowed from folk tradition and seen in other Morality plays, such as *Mankind*. In *Magnyfycence*, for example, we can find the characteristic calling for room:

CLOKED COLLUSION: Gyve this gentylman rome, syrs, stonde utter!

(l. 753)

As Richard Southern has noted, because the actors needed to make their entrances through the crowds of spectators, an entrance was often anticipated, so that room would be given to the actor attempting to come into the hall.[3] Stage directions for exits are very scarce, because an exit could be effected almost imperceptibly by merging with the crowd. The anticipated entrance and the calling attention to an entrance continued into the Elizabethan period and would be meaningless if this ancestry were not taken into account.

MEASURE: Nowe pleasyth you a lytell whyle to stande;
Me semeth Magnyfycence is comynge here at hande.

(ll. 161–2)

John Bale contributed plays to the popular repertory, writing plays for local actors who took to the road. He may have written for the Earl of Oxford's players early in his career and in the 1530s he wrote for Lord Cromwell's Players, until his patron fell from grace and Bale fled to the continent. His play *Three Laws* (1538) is the earliest extant play to have a casting list which shows how the doubling was to be achieved. Bale above all other early Tudor playwrights developed the use of doubling from an artless expedient into a craft to be mastered and exploited by the writer.

Bevington explains the doubling and its effect very clearly.[4] *Three Laws* has only one female character, Idolatry, who doubles with Law of Moses and Hypocrisy. The Vice figure Infidelity doubles with Prolocuter and Christian Faith, who provide the prologue and epilogue respectively. These roles were presumably those played by the leading actor, who introduces and apologises for his play, and who is then on stage for almost the entire performance as the Vice. It is not impossible that Bale himself as the creator of the piece would have been just such a leading actor, thus manipulating the main action. One of the other actors played God, while the others doubled three roles each, one of the Laws and two of the Vice's helpers. Trinities of various kinds appear in the play as the structural properties of the number three are played upon not only in the doubling but also in the stage action. The Three Laws are contested by a total of six enemies under a Vice figure, two assistants to each act of attempted subversion. In the final movement of the play the number three appears again in the three scourges of water, sword and fire used by God to destroy the Vice, Infidelity.

Sometimes the plays called for action to use different parts of the hall floor as differentiated locations. The poor visibility and crowded conditions made it possible for actors to initiate action in different locations simultaneously in the hall and to act as if they were unaware of each other's presence. The comic possibilities of a clash of speakers, whether in a hall or elsewhere, are brilliantly exploited by John Heywood in his play *The Pardoner and the Friar* (c. 1513–29). This fast-moving comedy begins with two introductory speeches attempting to catch the audience's attention, one delivered by the Friar and the other, possibly in a different part of the hall, by the Pardoner. It is not possible to tell from the printed copies of the play whether these speeches were spoken one after the other, as they are printed, or whether they did in fact go on simultaneously in a hilarious cacophony. As the two speakers become aware of each other they vie for the floor. In print their speeches appear in alternate lines. In performance it is possible to envisage an increasing crescendo of noise as each tries to shout down the other to hilarious effect. The punctuation of one speech by another makes nonsense of both, and, while the speeches are in couplets, while both are speaking the rhyme scheme becomes ab ab. They echo each other as they become increasingly irritated by the intrusion:

> P: Ay, by the mass – one cannot hear
> F: What a babbling maketh yonder fellow
> P: For the babbling of yonder foolish frere.[5]

This is comic writing of the highest order, disarmingly simple, yet brilliantly designed to deflate both characters.

From the mid-sixteenth century onward the staging methods of Hall drama change gradually and further staging features are used. The first item which requires comment is the use of the 'traverse', which provided a retiring place and may have been ancestor to the discovery space required by the Elizabethan theatre. This was most probably a pair of curtains, possibly hung in front of the screen between the doors. The next addition to the place of performance was the stage itself, first mention being made of this feature in the university drama, *Gammer Gurton's Needle*, which was performed at Christ's College, Cambridge in the mid-sixteenth century.

The elite drama to which *Gammer Gurton's Needle* belongs is different in several respects to the popular-based tradition so far discussed. Elite drama would have a number of possible spheres of influence, such as schools and universities, the Inns of Court, and the Royal Court. *Respublica* is a courtly Morality play, acted in the Christmas period of 1553. Typically, it was performed by boy actors, the Children of the Chapel Royal, and may have been written by their master Nicholas Udall. Unlike the popular plays it shows a knowledge of classical drama, as it displays a five-act structure and continental scene divisions. While it is based on a *Psychomachia*, the ideological combats are only verbal. There is no horseplay or ribaldry and it had highly elaborate costumes and scenery. There was no doubling; all eleven of the players appeared at once and there were a large number of female roles, facts which indicate that the play was intended for child actors and not for an adult professional troupe.[6] Sometimes the gentlemen of the Chapel also appeared in court entertainments, so court drama was not just performed by children. Court shows took many forms and how much the Interlude tradition was enriched by the elaborate pageantry of disguisings, masques, jousts and other forms of entertainment is difficult to measure.

School and university dramas all tend to a similar elaboration in casting and stage design, even when they deliberately use popular conventions. Plays such as *Ralph Roister Doister*, again by Udall, while displaying its educated auspices in a five-act classical structure, incorporated the popular drama's Vice figure in the person of Matthew Merrygreek.

In the earlier period of the popular Interlude the Vice has indisputable command of the stage and it is safe to assume that the leading actor usually portrayed the Vice. With the growth of secular characters in the plays the relationship between the Vice and the leading actor becomes less clearly defined. In the title character of *Hickscorner* we have the first use in a Morality of a name which is not explained as a personification, 'Hick' being a diminutive of the name Richard. The playwright is not concerned here with political allegory, but offers instead robust character sketches of known Tudor low-lifers. These characters differ from Morality play figures in their speech, which depends to a much greater degree on co-reference to create a shared world with shared assumptions and experiences outside the play world seen by the audience.

We can compare a passage in *Mankind* with one in *Hickscorner* to demonstrate the nature of the transition. Both talk of prison experience and the subject matter is entirely conventional. We will look at the *Mankind* passage first.

> MISCHIEF: here cometh a man of arms; why stande ye so still?
>   Of murder and manslaughter I haue my belly fill.
> NOWADAYS: What, Mischief! have ye been in prison?
>   and it be your will,
>   Meseemeth ye have sco(u)red a pair of fetters.
> MISCHIEF: I was chained by the arms; lo! I have them here.
>   The chains I brast asunder and killed the jailor,
>   Yea, and his fair wife halsed in a corner:
>   (ll. 639–46)

Notice in the exchange that the deictic, rather than the co-referential strategies, are to the fore in the discourse. The concentration is fixed upon objects within the place which are shown to the audience. Thus, we are told, 'Here cometh a man of arms', a pun stressing the chains and fetters on Mischief's arms as well as stressing person deixis, and 'lo! I have them here', stressing object deixis, as fetters and chains are held aloft. While reference outside, to the prison and the past action occurs, the stress is firmly placed on the physical scene in front of us – Mischief holding up his chains and fetters.

The passage from *Hickscorner* has the same subject matter, but the conversation rides more extensively on anaphora. There are references to 'that sort' and the question 'And what life have they there?'. These parts of the discourse only make sense as a result of the preceding conversation, as there is no one present to represent 'that sort' and no one within the place to whom the question refers.

> IMAG: Saw ye not of Hick Scorner?
> He promised me to come hither.
> FR. WILL: Why, sir, knowest thou him?
> IMAG: Yea, yea man, he is full nigh of my kin,
>   And in Newgate we dwelled together,
>   For he and I were both shackled in a fetter.
> FR. WILL: Sir, lay you beneath or high on the sollar?
> IMAG: Nay, iwis, among the thickest of yeomen of the collar.
>
> (ll. 232–9)

The quantity of time given in the play to this type of conversation is significant, as it explores talk, talkers and talking situations freely, presenting conversation as a specific kind of activity or interactivity, as the audience eavesdrop on details of the speakers' past lives. Reference through discourse to diegetic space – to places which are inscribed in the utterances – is extensive in this play. This encourages the audience to sense that the players have an existence in the diversified social scene of the England of their day, both outside and inside the place of the mimetic play space.

The use of time and place in this play contrasts with that observed in *The Castle of Perseverance* with its all-encompassing approach to deictic reference. Medieval inclusiveness has given way to specificity. Here, the combination of a contemporisation and individuation of characters, effected by the use of co-reference to give scope for the presentation of background information through conversation, leaves the audience free to be affected by this depiction of their times, without being implicated in the judgement on it.

The increasing use of anaphora to present a diversified, shared domain coincides with the attribution of greater realism to the drama. In the Tudor plays normative reality was increasingly portrayed as apart from, outside, the play world. This did not replace that celebratory reality of the communion of audience and play world. But rather than simply affirming the experience which was offered to them, as they would do with a Mystery or earlier Morality play, the audience were increasingly involved with characters and contexts independent of themselves and their own situation. These dramatists recognised the restrictiveness of the universal when reduced to the socially normative.

The secular human hero continues to grow from such discourse methods throughout the century. It is assumed that John Bale was responsible for the great leap forward of giving the dramatis personae of Morality plays an identity drawn from history, as no earlier example of this phenomenon is known. His *Kyng Johan* (1538) can thus be seen as a precursor to the Elizabethan Chronicle and History plays. In the 1560s *Horestes*, one of the 'mirror' plays, ambitiously staged battles, using the kind of staging gymnastics which anticipate the Elizabethan public stage. The play doubles twenty-seven roles for six players. There are two leads, the Vice and Horestes, who are doubled as little as possible, the four remaining actors carrying the rest of the roles. There is a great deal of slapstick and the muscularity of the Elizabethan public stage is prefigured here, with the Vice, for example, 'thwacking' other characters and then running around the stage as part of the fast-moving action.

The play requires a troupe of two leading players to take on the Vice and the hero, who divide the labour of the prologue and epilogue between them. The way has been prepared for the Elizabethan play troupes and their secular leading roles, Mucedorus, Hieronimo, Edward the Second, and Richard the Third.[7]

It will be clear that the status of the mimetic act has changed somewhat over the period we have been discussing. In this process there has been an addition to the idealist mimesis which accepts that there is ultimately a world more real than this phenomenal world. This addition is a mimesis concerned with expressing directly the experiences of this world as closely as possible. The tension generated by the co-existence of and differences between the two is something which enriches the Elizabethan stage, but this is properly the subject of another study.

To account for one's conflicts even as one offends needs a drama which interrogates by encompassing mimicry and presentation. It offers to the audience not just the pleasure of identification with the illusion of expressive personality, but also the knowledge which comes from the awareness of the show. This is the balance found in *Dr Faustus*, where the relationship between the individual person and the moral absolute is so effectively questioned.

Notes

Abbreviations Used

The following standard abbreviations have been used:
EETS – Early English Text Society
JEGP – Journal of English and Germanic Philology
PMLA – Publications of the Modern Language Association
REED – Records of Early English Drama

General Introduction

1. Hrotsvitha wrote a series of Latin plays in imitation of the comedies of Terence in the tenth century and Hildegard of Bingen wrote a dramatic Psychomachia which may be considered a precursor of the Morality play in the twelfth century. Cf. Richard Axton, *European Drama of the Early Middle Ages* (London, 1974), pp. 26–9 and Katherina M. Wilson, *Medieval Women Writers* (Manchester, 1984), pp. 30–63 and 109–130.

2. For texts and discussion of the Latin liturgical drama, cf. Karl Young, *The Drama of the Medieval Church*, 2 vols (Oxford, 1933/62). The Shrewsbury Fragments are printed in *Non-Cycle Plays and Fragments*, ed. Norman Davis, EETS, SS 1 (Oxford, 1970), pp. 1–7.

3. Translations of these plays are given in Richard Axton and John Stevens, *Medieval French Plays* (Oxford, 1971). This book also contains the translated texts of two twelfth-century Anglo-Norman plays, *Le Jeu d'Adam* and *La Seinte Resureccion*, which are thought to have been performed in England.

4. *Interludium de Clerico et Puella* in J. A. W. Bennett and G. V. Smithers (eds), *Early Middle English Verse and Prose* (Oxford, 1966/1974).

5. Cf. Alan Brody, *The English Mummers and their Plays* (London, 1970), and Axton, *European Drama*, pp. 33–44, 175–94 and 'Popular Modes in the Earliest Plays', in *Medieval Drama*, ed. Neville Denny, *Stratford-upon-Avon Studies*, 16 (London, 1973), pp. 10–39.

6. The texts of the Robin Hood Plays are available in R. B. Dobson

and J. Taylor, *Rymes of Robyn Hood: An Introduction to the English Outlaw* (London, 1976, repr. and rev. 1988). Cf. also David Wiles, *The Early Plays of Robin Hood* (Ipswich, 1981).

7. Cf. David L. Jeffrey, 'English Saints' Plays', in *Medieval Drama*, ed. Denny, pp. 69–89.

8. The plays of Mary Magdalene and St Paul are printed in *The Digby Plays*, Baker, Murphy and Hall (eds), EETS, 283 (Oxford, 1982) and in David Bevington, *Medieval Drama* (Boston, 1975).

9. The *Play of the Sacrament* is printed in *Non-Cycle Plays and Fragments*, ed. Davis, pp. 58–89 and in Bevington, *Medieval Drama*.

10. Cf. Glynne Wickham, *Early English Stages*, 3 vols, vol. 1 (2nd edn, London and New York, 1980), pp. 179–228. Details of royal entries to Coventry are given by Hardin Craig in his edition of the Coventry Plays, *Two Coventry Corpus Christi Plays*, ed. Hardin Craig, EETS, ES 87 (2nd edn, London, 1957, repr. 1967), pp. 109–18.

11. A. C. Cawley, *Everyman and Medieval Miracle Plays* (London, 1956/1974).

1. Mystery Plays

1. Cf. Alexandra F. Johnston, 'The Procession and Play of Corpus Christi in York after 1426', in *Leeds Studies in English*, NS, VII (1975), 55–62. Alan H. Nelson, in his *The Medieval English Stage* (Chicago, 1974), offers a different interpretation of the evidence with respect to the relationship between the procession and the plays.

2. Cf. V. A. Kolve, *The Play Called Corpus Christi* (Stanford, 1966), p. 51.

3. A cycle of Cornish plays has also survived in a slightly different form from the four English plays. The cycle is edited and translated by Markham Norris as *The Cornish Ordinalia* (Washington, DC, 1969).

4. The texts have survived of 49 plays but the manuscript also contains the title and pages left blank for a further two plays; the controversial 'Fergus' play mentioned in records has no surviving text.

5. Nelson, *Medieval English Stage*, and Martial Rose, *The Wakefield Mystery Plays* (London, 1961) are the principal opponents of true-processional staging. However, Nelson has since retracted his objections, which have also been effectively countered by Margaret Dorrell in her article, 'Two Studies of the York Corpus Christi Play', in *Leeds Studies in English*, NS, VI (1972), 63–111.

6. Cf. R. A. Beadle, *York Plays* (London, 1982), pp. 429–33 and 425–7.

7. See below, Chapter 5. The Mercers' Indenture is printed in Peter Happé (ed.), *Medieval English Drama* (London, 1984), pp. 29–30.

8. Cf. The Shearman and Taylors' Pageant, in Hardin Craig (ed.), *Two Coventry Corpus Christi Plays*, EETS, ES 87 (Oxford, 1957/67), ll. 204–25 and *Processus Noe*, in A. C. Cawley (ed.), *The Wakefield Pageants in the Towneley Cycle* (Manchester, 1958/71), ll. 370–2.

9. Cf. *Records of Early English Drama, Chester*, ed. Lawrence M.

Clopper (Toronto and Manchester, 1979), pp. 81–4, 91–3, 106–108.

10. Cf. Meg Twycross, 'Transvestism in the Mystery Plays', in *Medieval English Theatre*, 5.2 (1983), 123–80.

11. Cf. Richard Rastall, '"Alle Hefne Makyth Melody"', in Paula Neuss (ed.), *Aspects of Early English Drama* (Cambridge, 1983), pp. 1–12.

12. Cf. *A Tretise of Miraclis Pleyinge*, a fourteenth-century Wycliffite attack on the plays, printed in Happé, *Medieval English Drama*, p. 27.

13. Cf. Beadle, *York Plays*, p. 32 and Nelson, *Medieval English Stage*, p. 47.

14. Cf. Nelson, *Medieval English Stage*, p. 139 and Hardin Craig, *Two Coventry Corpus Christi Plays*, xxiii. Cf. also the arguments used by the Norwich Guild of St Luke for assistance in the production of their pageants in 1527 in Norman Davis (ed.), *Non-Cycle Plays and Fragments*, EETS, SS 1 (Oxford, 1970), xxvii.

15. Cf. Alan D. Justice, 'Trade Symbolism in the York Cycle', in *Theatre Journal*, xxxi (March 1979), 47–58 and Beadle, *York Plays*, p. 30.

16. Cf. Nelson *Medieval English Stage*, pp. 63–4. For a full treatment of the suppression of the Mystery Cycles see H. C. Gardiner, *Mysteries' End* (New Haven, 1946).

17. Eleanor Prosser, *Drama and Religion in the English Mystery Plays* (Stanford, 1961). Under the auspices of the University of Toronto, the REED (Records of Early English Drama) series has been set up 'to locate, transcribe and publish systematically all surviving external evidence of dramatic, ceremonial, and minstrel activity in Great Britain before 1642'. The first volume in the series, the York records, appeared in 1979 and since then the volumes on Chester, Coventry, Newcastle and other cities have been issued.

18. Two individual Abraham and Isaac Plays survive, one mid-fifteenth century, probably from the Northampton area and one late fifteenth century, probably from the Brome, Norfolk, area. However, these two locations have no indications of having cycle productions. The plays are printed in Norman Davis, *Non-Cycle Plays*, pp. 32–42, 43–57.

2. N-Town 'Cain and Abel'

1. N-Town Plays, published as *Ludus Coventriae*, ed. K. S. Block, EETS, ES 120 (London, 1922, repr. 1960/1974), ll. 525–7.

2. The true Coventry Cycle is published as *Two Coventry Corpus Christi Plays*, ed. Hardin Craig, EETS, ES 87, 2nd edn (London, 1957, repr. 1967).

3. Hardin Craig, in his *English Religious Drama* (Oxford, 1955), pp. 265–80 and 'The Lincoln Cordwainers' Pageant', *PMLA*, xxxii (1917), 605–15, assembled evidence for Lincoln as the home of the N-Town Cycle and since then Kenneth Cameron and Stanley J. Kahrl have argued the case with more evidence and carefully worked out staging possibilities for the cycle in Lincoln in 'The N-Town Plays at Lincoln', *Theatre Notebook*, xx (ii) (1965), 61–9 and 'Staging the N-Town Cycle', *Theatre Notebook*,

xxi (1967), 122–38, 152–65.

4. N-Town Cain and Abel Play, in A. C. Cawley (ed.), *Everyman and Medieval Miracle Plays* (London, 1956, repr. 1974), pp. 25–33, ll. 75–8. Henceforth referred to as *Cain and Abel*.

5. 'Cayne, husbandes crafte thou must goe to; / And Abel, a shepharde bee' (Chester, Play II, ll. 475–6). The Towneley-Wakefield play does not present Abel as a shepherd but shows him offering sheaves of corn as sacrifice as Cain does.

6. Cf. Eleanor Prosser, *Drama and Religion in the English Mystery Plays* (Stanford, 1961), pp. 67–88. Prosser's discussion of the role of comedy in the Mystery plays is very useful.

7. For the possibilities of masks being used in the Mystery plays, cf. Meg Twycross and Sarah Carpenter, 'Masks in the Medieval Theatre', *Medieval English Theatre*, 3.1 (1981), 29–36, reprinted as 'Purposes and Effects of Masking' in Peter Happé (ed.), *Medieval English Drama* (London, 1986), pp. 171–9. Cf. also the details of the properties of the York Last Judgement Play, Chapter 5 below and also Happé, pp. 29–30.

8. This continuation of the Cain and Abel Play is not included in the version given by Cawley in *Everyman and Medieval Miracle Plays*.

9. For other uses of this routine, cf. Gustave Cohen, 'La scène de l'Aveugle et de son valet dans le théâtre français du moyen âge', *Romania*, xli (1912), 345–72.

10. Cf. Oliver F. Emerson, 'Legends of Cain, especially in Old and Middle English', *PMLA*, xxi (1906), 831–929.

11. Cf. Justice, 'Trade Symbolism', p. 57.

3. Townley-Wakefield 'Secunda Pastorum'

1. Cf. A. C. Cawley, *The Wakefield Pageants in the Towneley Cycle* (Manchester, 1958), pp. xiv–xv for precise details of the references to Wakefield contained in the plays.

2. Cf. ibid., Appendix 1 and Jean Forrester and A. C. Cawley, 'The Corpus Christi Play of Wakefield: a New Look at the Wakefield Burgess Court Records', *Leeds Studies in English*, NS, 7 (1974), 108–16.

3. Martial Rose in his *The Wakefield Mystery Plays* (London, 1961), argues for a fixed-stage method of representation. The Wakefield Festival production of the Cycle in 1980, directed by Jane Oakshott, adapted a combination of the two methods by using a series of fixed scaffolds and letting the actors for each individual play 'process' from one scaffold to the next.

4. Cf. Hans-Jürgen Diller, 'The Craftsmanship of the Wakefield Master', *Anglia*, lxxxiii (1965), 271–88, repr. in Jerome Taylor and Alan H. Nelson (eds), *Medieval English Drama: Essays Critical and Contextual* (Chicago and London, 1972), pp. 245–59, for an analysis of the Wakefield Master's style.

5. For a full list of the folk-tale analogues to the Mak story cf. Robert C. Cosbey, 'The Mak Story and its Folklore Analogues', *Speculum*, xx (1945), 310–17.

6. A. C. Cawley, *The Wakefield Pageants in the Towneley Cycle, Prima Pastorum*, ll. 60–3; Cawley, *Everyman and Medieval Miracle Plays, Secunda Pastorum*, ll. 15–18, 37–45.

7. Cf. V. J. Scattergood, *Politics and Poetry in the Fifteenth Century* (London, 1971), p. 360. Cf. also R. H. Robbins, *Historical Poems of the XIVth and XVth Centuries* (New York, 1959), p. 147 for a fifteenth-century poem which is very similar to the *Prima Pastorum* Shepherd's complaint.

8. Cf. John Speirs, 'The Mystery Cycle (I) Some Towneley Cycle Plays', *Scrutiny*, XVIII (1951–2), 86–117.

9. The first quotation is from the Chester Shepherds Play (ll. 250–1) and the second from the Netley Abbey Mummers' Play, printed in Alan Brody, *The English Mummers and their Plays* (London, 1970), pp. 131–6, esp. p. 132. For other instances of folk drama borrowings in the Mystery plays, cf. Richard Axton, *European Drama of the Early Middle Ages* (London, 1974), pp. 38–9,175–82.

10. *Interludium de Clerico et Puella*, printed in J. A. W. Bennett and G. V. Smithers (eds), *Early Middle English Verse and Prose* (Oxford, 1966/1974), pp. 196–200. Cf. also Axton, *European Drama*, p. 21.

11. Cf. Homer A. Watt, 'The Dramatic Unity of the *Secunda Pastorum*', in *Essays and Studies in Honor of Carleton Brown* (New York, 1940), pp. 158–66 and F. J. Thompson, 'Unity in *The Second Shepherds' Tale*', *Modern Language Notes*, LXIV (1949), 302–6 for further discussion of the parallels in the two sections of the play.

12. 'The homeliness of the Wakefield Shepherds' gifts is realistically appropriate to the rustic Shepherds and to the poverty of the Divine Family. But although apparently as simple as those in earlier Shepherds' [sic] plays, these become, as attributes of the Christ Child, luminously significant. . . . Above all, they designate the child as the Christ by manifesting, as symbols of offered faith, his sacrificial manhood, spiritual primacy, and lordship and power.' (Lawrence J. Ross, 'Symbol and Structure in *Secunda Pastorum*', repr. in Taylor and Nelson, *Medieval English Drama*, pp. 177–211, p. 197).

4. York 'Crucifixion Play'

1. The document, known as the Mercers' Indenture, is printed in Happé, *Medieval English Drama*, pp. 29–30.

2. Cf. Nelson, *Medieval English Stage* and Rose, *Wakefield Mystery Plays*. For refutations of Nelson, cf. Alexandra Johnston's review of Nelson, *The Medieval English Stage* in *University of Toronto Quarterly*, XLIV (1975), 238–48 and Margaret Dorrell, 'Two Studies of the York Corpus Christi Play', *Leeds Studies in English*, NS, VI (1972), 63–111.

3. Alexandra Johnston and Margaret Rogerson (eds), *REED York*, 2 vols (Toronto and Manchester, 1979), II, p. 722.

4. Ibid., p. 723.

5. Cf. Clifford Davidson, 'The Realism of the York Realist and the York Passion Play', *Speculum*, 50 (1975), 270–83, reprinted in Happé,

Medieval English Drama, pp. 101–17.

6. Cf. V. A. Kolve, *The Play Called Corpus Christi* (Stanford, 1966), pp. 101–23 for a discussion of 'God's time' and how it works in the cycle plays.

7. Nicholas Love, *Mirrour of the Blessyd Lyf of Jesu Christ*, Sig. N3ᵛ, cited in Davidson, 'Realism of the York Realist', p. 112.

8. Cf. Davidson, 'Realism of the York Realist', for an exposition of this movement and the relation of the Mystery plays to movements in the visual arts in the fifteenth century.

9. Wycliffe considered this immediacy of the drama a particularly blasphemous quality in representing Christian history and disapproved of it. Cf. the anonymous Wycliffite Treatise 'against miracles playing' (*A Tretise of Miraclis Pleyinge*), reprinted in Happé, *Medieval English Drama*, p. 27.

10. It should be remembered that in the edition of the play in *Everyman and Medieval Miracle Plays* the stage directions have been supplied by A. C. Cawley.

11. Cf. Johnston and Rogerson, *REED, York*, pp. 22,707.

12. Cf. J. W. Robinson, 'The Art of the York Realist', in Taylor and Nelson, *Medieval English Drama*, pp. 230–44.

13. Cf. Kolve, *Play Called Corpus Christi*, chapter 9 and Lawrence M. Clopper, 'Tyrants and Villains: Characterization in the Passion Sequence of the English Cycle Plays', *Modern Language Quarterly*, 41 (1980), 3–20.

14. Cf. Chester, XVIA, The Ironmongers' Play, ll. 382–3,398–9:

> What I doe I may not see
> whether yt be evell or good
> . . .
> Of mercye, lord, I thee nowe praye
> for I wyste not what I did.

5. Chester 'Last Judgement Play'

1. Prior to *c*.1519 there is a reference to the Corpus Christi play contained in a dispute between the Coopers and the Ironmongers over their responsibilities for the Scourging and Crucifixion Play in 1421–2. Cf. Lawrence M. Clopper, 'The Rogers' Description of the Chester Plays', *Leeds Studies in English*, NS, vii (1974), 63–94 and 'The History and Development of the Chester Cycle', *Modern Philology*, 75 (1977–8), 219–46 and *REED Chester*, ed. Clopper (Toronto and Manchester, 1979), Introduction.

2. Cf. Clopper, 'History and Development of the Chester Cycle', p. 222.

3. Cf. Clopper, 'The Rogers' Description of the Chester Plays', p. 73. The Rogers' description of the Chester Pageant wagons is given in Happé,

Medieval English Drama, pp. 30–1. Copies of the four versions of the *Brevary* are in *REED Chester*; sections on the plays, pp. 238–52, 324–6, 355, 435–6.

4. All quotations are from R. M. Lumiansky and David Mills (eds), *The Chester Mystery Cycle*, EETS, SS 3 (Oxford, 1974). Cf. also ll. 515–16, 529–30, 549–50, 557–8, 568, 579–80.

5. *The Towneley Plays*, George England and A. W. Pollard (eds), EETS, ES 71 (Oxford, 1897/1952), Play XXX, ll. 350–8.

6. The Chester stage direction following line 356 gives 'Stabunt angeli cum cruce, corona spinea, lancea, et instrumentis aliis; ipsa demonstrant'.

7. The Mercers' Indenture is printed in Happé, *Medieval English Drama*, pp. 29–30.

8. See reference to Titivillus in *Mankind*, Chapter 8 below.

9. This is certainly suggested by the Mercers' Indenture which lists 'Array' for the 'euell soules' separately from 'Array' for the 'gode saules'.

10. Cf. *Le Mistere d'Adam* in Axton and Stevens (eds), *Medieval French Plays*, pp. 1–44, esp. p. 36 and the illustration of the Valenciennes *hourdement* which shows a smoking Hell, printed in Taylor and Nelson, *Medieval English Drama*, p. 123 and on the front cover of the paperback edition.

11. Cf. David J. Leigh, 'The Doomsday Mystery Play: An Eschatological Morality', *Modern Philology*, LXVII (1969–70), 211–23, repr. in Taylor and Nelson, *Medieval English Drama*, pp. 260–78.

6. Didactic Drama: 'Everyman' and other Morality Plays

1. The phrase is used as a section heading by the scholar Glynne Wickham. Cf. Glynne Wickham, *The Medieval Stage* (London, 1974), p. 162.

2. These tracts are discussed, with illustrative reproductions in Bertram Joseph, *Elizabethan Acting* (Oxford, 1951).

3. A. C. Cawley (ed.), *Everyman* (Manchester, 1961), has an excellent introduction to the play. Cf. in particular pp. xx–xxviii.

4. *The Pride of Life* in *Non-Cycle Plays and Fragments*, ed. Norman Davis, EETS SS, 1 (Oxford, 1970), pp. 90–105, ll. 80–8.

5. The quotations given here are taken from Thomas à Kempis, *The Imitation of Christ*, ed. and trans. Leo Sherley-Price (Harmondsworth, 1952), pp. 58–9, 194.

6. William Langland, *Piers Plowman, C-Text*, ed. Derek Pearsall (London, 1978), p. 130. There are many other examples of similar anti-clerical statements in all three of the *Piers Plowman* texts.

7. Julian of Norwich, *The Revelation of Divine Love*, ed. and trans. Clifton Walters (Harmondsworth, 1966), pp. 89–90.

8. R. T. Davies (ed.), *Medieval English Lyrics* (London, 1963), p. 279.

9. Robert Potter, *The English Morality Play* (London, 1975), p. 54.

10. Ibid., pp. 222–4.

11. Bertolt Brecht, *Seven Plays by Bertolt Brecht*, ed. Eric Bentley (New York, 1961), p. xi.

7. The Place

1. *Athaneum*, 20 July 1901, p. 103.

2. It seems likely that the Nativity Play and the Shepherds Play and the Herod and the Magi Play were performed 'in tandem' in the York Cycle. Cf. Chapter 1, note 6 above.

3. Michael Issacharoff, 'Space and Reference in Drama', *Poetics Today*, 2/3 (1981), 211–24. This article contains many of the essential ideas about space which are explored here in relation to *The Castle of Perseverance*. A similar approach is also found in Keir Elam, *The Semiotics of Theatre and Drama* (London, 1980), pp. 62 ff.

4. Richard Southern, *The Medieval Theatre in the Round* (London, 1957). This was an extremely important book in the consideration of medieval theatre by scholars and changed the whole nature of debate, allowing Morality plays to be regarded as serious artistic forms rather than merely of antiquarian interest.

5. Cf. ibid. Plates 2, 3, 4 and 5. The picture is also reproduced in Taylor and Nelson (eds.), *Medieval English Drama: Essays Critical and Contextual* (Chicago and London, 1972), p. 85.

6. Natalie Crohn Schmitt, 'Was There a Medieval Theatre in the Round? A Re-examination of the Evidence', *Theatre Notebook*, 23 (1968–9), 130–42, and 24 (1969–70), 18–25, reprinted in Taylor and Nelson, *Medieval English Drama*, pp. 292–315. References in this chapter are to the reprinted version.

7. Cf. *Castle* diagram illustration.

8. H. R. L. Beadle, *Medieval Drama in East Anglia* (University of York DPhil thesis, 1977), cf. in particular Chapter 6. An account of the game place at Walsham is quoted from the *Field Book of Walsham le Willows* in Kenneth M. Dodd, 'Another Elizabethan Theatre in the Round', *Shakespeare Quarterly*, 21 (1970), 125–56.

9. John R. Elliot Jr, 'Medieval Rounds and Wooden Os: The Medieval Heritage of the Elizabethan Theatre', in *Medieval Drama*, ed. Neville Denny, *Stratford-upon-Avon Studies*, 16 (London, 1973), pp. 221–46, esp. p. 224.

10. A. Forstater and J. L. Baird, 'Mankind's Opening Speech', *Theatre Notebook*, 26 (1971–2), 60–2.

11. E. T. Schell, 'On the Imitation of Life's Pilgrimage in *The Castle of Perseverance*', *JEGP* (1969–70), 68, 235–48.

12. John Lyons, *Semantics*, 2 vols (Cambridge, London and New York, 1977), Vol. 2, pp. 718 ff.

13. The picture *Death and the Miser* by Hieronymous Bosch is now held at the National Gallery of Art, Washington DC, USA. It is reproduced in Taylor and Nelson, *Medieval English Drama*, p. 293.

8. Audience and Performance

1. Neville Denny, 'Aspects of the Staging of *Mankind*', *Medium Aevum*, 43 (1974), 52–63. Also of interest in this context is Richard Axton, *European Drama of the Early Middle Ages* (London, 1974), pp. 200–10.
2. Alan Brody, *The English Mummers and their Plays* (London, 1969), pp. 48 ff.
3. J. L. Austin in J. O. Urmson and Marina Sbisà (eds), *How To Do Things with Words: The William James Lectures delivered at Harvard University, 1955* (Oxford, 1962).
4. J. Q. Adams, *Chief Pre-Shakespearean Dramas* (Boston, 1924), pp. 345, 359. The first quotation is from the Oxfordshire *St George Play*, and the second from the Revesby *Sword Play*.
5. Mikhail Bakhtin, *Rabelais and his World* (Cambridge, Mass. and London, 1968). This book contains the fullest account of Bakhtin's ideas on Carnival.
6. John R. Searle, *Speech Acts: An Essay in the Philosophy of Language* (London and New York, 1969), p. 59.
7. A. Brandeis (ed.), *Jacob's Well*, EETS OS, 115 (London, 1900). Reference is made to this text in a very useful and interesting article by Paula Neuss, 'Active and Idle Language: Dramatic Images in *Mankind*', in Neville Denny (ed.), *Medieval Drama*, *Stratford-upon-Avon Studies*, 16 (London, 1973), pp. 42–67.

9. Signifying Practices

1. David M. Bevington, *Tudor Drama and Politics* (Cambridge, Mass., 1968), pp. 28–31.
2. Ibid., p. 44.
3. William Dodd, 'Meta-language and Character in Drama', *Lingua e stile*, 14/1 (1979), 135–50, esp. 141. A seminal work on meta-language is Louis Hjemslev, *Prolegomena to a Theory of Language*, (Madison, University of Wisconsin Press, 1943), cf. in particular p. 119.
4. Henry Medwall in F. S. Boas and A. W. Reed (eds), *Fulgens and Lucrece*, (London, 1926), p. xxii.
5. Dodd, 'Meta-language', p. 144.
6. Norman Davis (ed.), *Non-Cycle Plays and Fragments*, University of Leeds School of English Medieval Drama Facsimiles, 5 (Leeds, 1979), contains a text of *Doctrine Occupation and Idleness*.
7. Michel Foucault, *On The Order of Things*, (1966, current English edn, Tavistock, 1985).

10. Popular and Elite: the Legacy

1. Articles and books offering different views of the development of the Elizabethan Playhouse are Richard Hoseley, 'The Origins of the Shakespearean Playhouse', in *Shakespeare 400*, ed. J. McManaway (New

York, 1964) and C. Walter Hodges, *The Globe Restored* (London, 1953) as well as John R. Elliott Jr, 'Medieval Rounds and Wooden Os: The Medieval Heritage of Elizabethan Theatre', in Neville Denny (ed.), *Medieval Drama, Stratford-upon-Avon Studies*, 16 (London, 1973), pp. 223–46.

2. David M. Bevington, *From Mankind to Marlowe* (Cambridge Mass., 1962), pp. 68 ff.

3. Richard Southern, *The Staging of Plays before Shakespeare* (London, 1973), pp. 45 ff.

4. Bevington, *Mankind to Marlowe*, pp. 129–31.

5. John Heywood, *The Works of John Heywood*, in J. S. Farmer (ed.), *Early English Dramatists*, vol. 3 (London, 1903), p. 19.

6. Bevington, *Mankind to Marlowe*, pp. 82–3. See also David M. Bevington, 'Popular and Courtly Traditions on the Early Tudor Stage' in Denny (ed.), *Medieval Drama*, pp. 91–107, esp. p. 106.

7. Ibid.

Select Bibliography

MYSTERY PLAYS BIBLIOGRAPHY

Plays

Everyman and Medieval Miracle Plays, ed. A. C. Cawley (London, 1956, repr. 1974).

York Plays, ed. R. A. Beadle (London, 1982).

Richard Beadle and Pamela M. King (eds), *York Mystery Plays: A Selection in Modern Spelling* (Oxford, 1984).

David Bevington, *Medieval Drama* (Boston, 1975). Contains a selection from the Mystery Cycles, liturgical plays, twelfth-century drama, *The Conversion of St. Paul, Mary Magdalene, The Play of the Sacrament*, and a selection of Morality plays and Interludes.

Ludus Coventriae, ed. K. S. Block, EETS, ES 120 (London, 1922, repr. 1960/1974).

The Wakefield Pageants in the Towneley Cycle, ed. A. C. Cawley (Manchester, 1958/71).

Two Coventry Corpus Christi Plays, ed. Hardin Craig, EETS, ES 87 (Oxford, 1957/67).

Non-Cycle Plays and Fragments, ed. Norman Davis, EETS, SS 1 (Oxford, 1970).

The Towneley Plays, George England and A. U. Pollard (eds), EETS, ES 71 (Oxford, 1897/1952).

The Chester Mystery Cycle, R. M. Lumiansky and David Mills (eds), EETS, SS 3 (Oxford, 1974).

The Cornish Ordinalia, ed. and trans. Markham Norris, (Washington DC, 1969).

Richard Axton and John Stevens (eds), *Medieval French Plays* (Oxford, 1971).

J. A. W. Bennett and G. V. Smithers (eds), *Early Middle English Verse and Prose* (Oxford, 1966/1974).

R. B. Dobson and J. Taylor, *Rymes of Robyn Hood: An Introduction to*

167

the English Outlaw (London, 1976, repr. and rev. 1988).
David Wiles, *The Early Plays of Robin Hood* (Ipswich, 1981).

Records of Performance

Lawrence M. Clopper (ed.), *Records of Early English Drama, Chester* (Toronto and Manchester, 1979).
Alexandra Johnston and Margaret Rogerson (eds), *Records of Early English Drama, York*, 2 vols (Toronto and Manchester, 1979).
Ian Lancashire, *Dramatic Texts and Records of Britain: A Chronological Topography to 1558* (Toronto and Cambridge, 1984).

Criticism

Richard Axton, *European Drama of the Early Middle Ages* (London, 1974).
Alan Brody, *The English Mummers and their Plays* (London, 1970).
Neville Denny (ed.), *Medieval Drama, Stratford-upon-Avon Studies*, 16 (London, 1973).
H. C. Gardiner, *Mysteries' End* (New Haven, 1946).
Peter Happé (ed.), *Medieval English Drama* (London, 1984).
Stanley J. Kahrl, *Traditions of Medieval English Drama* (London, 1974).
V. A. Kolve, *The Play Called Corpus Christi* (Stanford, 1966).
Alan H. Nelson, *The Medieval English Stage* (Chicago, 1974).
Eleanor Prosser, *Drama and Religion in the English Mystery Plays* (Stanford, 1961).
Martial Rose, *The Wakefield Mystery Plays* (London, 1961).
Jerome Taylor and Alan H. Nelson (eds), *Medieval English Drama: Essays Critical and Contextual* (Chicago and London, 1972).
Glynne Wickham, *The Medieval Theatre* (London, 1974/1980).
Rosemary Woolf, *The English Mystery Plays* (London, 1972).

MORALITY PLAYS BIBLIOGRAPHY

Plays

Five Pre-Shakespearean Comedies, ed. F. S. Boas (London, Oxford and New York, 1970). Contains *Fulgens et Lucres, Ralph Roister Doister, Gammer Gurton's Needle* and *Supposes.*
Everyman and Medieval Miracle Plays, ed. A. C. Cawley (London, 1956 repr. 1974). Contains *Everyman* and a selection from the Mystery Cycle plays.
Tudor Interludes, ed. Peter Happé (Harmondsworth, 1972). Contains *Pride of Life, Mankind.*
Four Morality Plays, ed. Peter Happé (Harmondsworth, 1979). Contains *The Castle of Perseverance, Magnyfycence, King Johan, Ane Satire of the Thrie Estaitis.*

Two Tudor Interludes. ed. Ian Lancashire (Manchester, 1980). Contains *Youth* and *Hickscorner*.
English Moral Interludes, ed. Glynne Wickham (London, 1976). Contains *Mankind, Fulgens and Lucres, The Conversion of Saint Paul, The Temptation of our Lord, Nice Wanton, The Marriage Between Wit and Wisdom.*

Criticism

Richard Axton, *European Drama of the Early Middle Ages* (London, 1974).
David M. Bevington, *From Mankind to Marlowe* (London, 1962).
David M. Bevington, *Tudor Drama and Politics* (London, 1968).
A. C. Cawley, M. Jones, P. F. McDonald and D. Mills, *The Revels History of Drama in English*, vol. 1 (London, 1983).
T. W. Craik, *The Tudor Interlude* (Leicester, 1958).
T. W. Craik, L. Potter, N. Sanders and R. Southern, *The Revels History of Drama*, vol. 2 (London, 1980).
Neville Denny (ed.), *Medieval Drama, Stratford-upon-Avon Studies* 16 (London, 1973).
G. R. Owst, *Literature and Pulpit in Medieval England* (Oxford, 1961).
Robert Potter, *The English Morality Play* (London, 1975).
Richard Southern, *Medieval Theatre in the Round* (London, 1957).
Richard Southern, *The Staging of Plays before Shakespeare* (London, 1973).
Jerome Taylor and Alan H. Nelson (eds), *Medieval English Drama.* (London, 1972).
Glynne Wickham, *The Medieval Theatre* (London, 1974/80).

Chronological Table

Medieval Plays		Other Literature	Monarchs	Historical Events
	Medieval Plays			Edward III (1327–77)	
c. 1290–1335	Interludium de Clerico et Puella			
c. 1350	Pride of Life	Sir Gawain & the Green Knight (1350–1400?)		
		Piers Plowman (c. 1362)		Peasants' Revolt (1381)
1376	York Cycle (1st mention)	Canterbury Tales (c. 1387)	Richard II (1377–99)	
1392	Coventry Cycle (1st mention)			
1400–25	The Castle of Perseverance	fl. Gower (c. 1385–1408)	Henry IV (1399–1413)	
1422	Chester Cycle (1st mention)		Henry V (1413–22)	Battle of Agincourt (1415)
1427–1589	Newcastle Noah Play	fl. Lydgate (1416–49)	Henry VI (1422–61)	Wars of Roses (1455–85)
c. 1450	Towneley-Wakefield Cycle			
c. 1450–75	N-Town Cycle			
1460–63	Wisdom		Edward IV (1461–70)	
1461–1520	The Play of the Sacrament		Henry VI (1470–71)	
1465–70	Mankind		Edward IV (1471–83)	
1475	Robin Hood and the Sheriff of Nottingham			Caxton printing in England (1476)
1480–1520	Mary Magdalene and The Conversion of St Paul		Edward V (1483)	Discovery of America (1492)
			Richard III (1483–85)	
1495	Everyman		Henry VII (1485–1509)	
1497	Fulgens & Lucres			
c. 1507–8	Mundus et Infans			
1513	Youth			
c. 1513–21	The Pardoner & the Friar			
1514	Hickscorner	Utopia (1516)		

Medieval Plays	Other Literature	Monarchs	Historical Events
		Henry VIII (1509–47)	
1522 Magnificence			Break with Roman Church (1531)
1529 Play of Love			
1530 Norwich Cycle performed in Pentecost week			
1536 King Johan			
1538 The Temptation of our Lord			
1538 The Three Laws			
1539 Wit and Science			
c. 1547–8 Ralph Roister Doister		Edward VI (1547–53)	
1550 Nice Wanton			
1552 Ane Satire of the Thrie Estaitis			
1553 Gammer Gurton's Needle		Mary (1553–58)	
1553 Republica		Elizabeth I (1558–1603)	
1560 Robin Hood and the Friar and Robin Hood and the Potter			
1562 Gorboduc			
1564 Last performance Norwich Plays	Shakespeare (1564–1616)		
1567 Horestes	*Comedy of Errors* *Taming of the Shrew* *Two Gentlemen of Verona* *Henry VI* *Richard III* *King John* *Timon of Athens* } c. 1584–1592		
1569 Last performance York Cycle			
1569 Cambises	Marlowe (1564–93)		
1570 Misogonus	*Tamburlaine* 1587		
c. 1575 The Marriage between Wit and Wisdom			
1575 Last performance Chester Cycle			
1576 Last performance Wakefield Plays	*Doctor Faustus* *Edward II* *Jew of Malta* } 1589–90		
1590 Sir Thomas More			

Index

172